MIRACLE PETS

True Tales of Courage and Survival

Allan Zullo

Scholastic Inc.
New York Toronto London Auckland
Sydney Mexico City New Delhi Hong Kong

To my grandson, Daschel, with the hope that, when faced
with a difficult challenge, he never gives up.
—A.Z.

ISBN 978-0-545-25507-3

12 11 10 9 8 7 6 5 4 3 2   11 12 13 14 15 16/0

Printed in the U.S.A.   40
First Scholastic printing, September 2011

Contents

Never Say Die

Like humans, every animal possesses a survival instinct that takes over when facing a life-or-death situation. Whether that instinct is triggered by a predator or by thirst, hunger, cold, heat, pain, or terror, an animal will try something—anything—to live another day.

This book is a celebration of true cases of pets and wild animals that survived what appeared to be hopeless predicaments. You'll read, for example, about the survival of the dachshund that was snatched by an eagle, but fought back in a midair struggle; the cat that was trapped for two months under a concrete floor of a building under construction; the small water buffalo that was being pulled in a tug-of-war between a crocodile and a pride of lions.

Some animals took matters into their own paws, such as the cat that was hit by a car and left for dead, but endured a week of subfreezing temperatures while crawling home with two broken legs; the two pigs that escaped from a sausage factory, squeezed through a hole in a fence, leaped into an icy river, and swam to freedom; the family dog that ended up a castaway on a deserted island for four months.

Animal survivor stories like these offer an inspiring lesson that no matter the situation—however bleak, however desperate—there is always hope. Life is too precious to give up without a fight. If the survivors featured in this book had a motto, it would be this: Never say die!

Back from the Dead

A GRAVE SITUATION

Dogs have come back from the grave—literally.

In 1990, a four-year-old Jack Russell terrier named Mugsy was hit by a car in front of the house of his owner, Viola Tiszl, of Severna Park, Maryland. Although Viola was not home at the time, her boyfriend, Glenn Maloney, was there taking care of her children, Megan, five, and Kevin, three.

As soon as he heard the screeching of the tires, Maloney looked out the window and saw that Mugsy had been struck. He ordered the kids to stay in the house and then he dashed outside to see if the dog was still alive. "I picked Mugsy up, but he died in my arms," he told reporters later.

Maloney carried the body to the backyard and dug a hole three feet deep and buried Mugsy. "I know a dead dog when I see one," he recalled. "This one was real dead. He was not breathing. He had no heartbeat."

That evening, after she came home from work, Tiszl and Maloney took the children out back to view the grave. Megan said a prayer, and the family decided they would put a wooden cross on the burial site the next morning.

At 5:30 A.M. — about 14 hours after Mugsy had been buried — Tiszl and Maloney were awakened by a scratching noise at the back door. "I couldn't believe it," recalled Maloney. "[There was Mugsy with his] little tail wagging ninety miles an hour!"

Mugsy was covered with dirt and his eyes were bloodshot, but otherwise he seemed in excellent shape.

Tiszl attributed the dog's astounding recovery to his breeding. "Jack Russells are bred to burrow after foxes," she said. "I guess when he woke up in that hole, he just thought it was another old hole and he dug his way out, not knowing it was supposed to be his grave."

Brownie, a small, tan mutt, also made a dramatic return from the "dead" four years later.

The dog had fallen asleep behind the family pickup truck. Not knowing Brownie was there, owner Mary Bratcher, of Artesia, New Mexico, backed up the truck and accidentally ran over him.

Breaking down in tears, Bratcher lifted her limp pet and looked for any sign of life, but she found none. "His chest went up and down twice, and then he stopped breathing," she recalled. "I thought he was dead."

Not wanting her children to see their lifeless dog, Bratcher had her brother carry Brownie to a nearby field and bury the beloved pet in a three-foot-deep grave. "I told the kids that Brownie had gone to heaven," she said.

Late the next afternoon, Bratcher returned from a trip to the store and screamed in shock. Lying by the front porch steps was none other than Brownie himself! He was shivering from the cold, caked in dirt, and not breathing well. Bratcher rushed him to the veterinarian, who treated the dog for a rib injury, a broken leg, and a concussion. The most serious problem was that Brownie lost his right eye. But otherwise, he made a full recovery.

Looie the Maltese-poodle mix missed his own cremation by a whisker.

One snowy night in 1990, the frisky, black, eight-year-old pooch managed to squeeze out of the backyard gate of the home of his owner, Martin Heimlich, of Salt Lake City, Utah. As Heimlich chased after Looie, the dog darted into a busy street, where he was struck by a minivan, then by a car, and finally by another auto.

The horror-stricken Heimlich sprinted out into the heavy traffic and picked up his apparently lifeless dog. The owner checked his pet but could not detect any breathing or a heartbeat.

"The whole family was in shock," recalled Heimlich. "We were grieving, certain that we'd lost Looie."

He had planned to bury his pooch, but record low temperatures had frozen the ground. So he put Looie in a box outside on the porch and called the animal-control office to pick up the dog and cremate him. The pet was left in the box for two days.

"On the morning that his body was to be picked up, I couldn't resist taking one last peek," said Heimlich. "So I opened the box, and he looked up at me. I said to myself, 'Dead dogs don't look up at you.' Then [Looie] wobbled his head. And I said, 'Dead dogs don't move.' I reached down and found his heart was pounding, and he was warm."

Thrilled beyond belief, Heimlich took Looie to the Central Valley Veterinary Hospital, where the dog was operated on for a fractured hind leg, ruptured ear drum, and eye injuries. Although he lost his left eye, Looie recovered from his near-tragedy.

"Looie just refused to die," said Heimlich. "Obviously, it wasn't his time to go."

SURPRISE SURVIVOR

A never-say-die cat was found alive in the rubble of a flattened house in Taiwan almost 80 days after the island country was rocked by a devastating earthquake.

The quake, which measured between 7.3 and 7.6 on the Richter scale, struck on September 21, 1999, killing 2,368 people, seriously injuring more than 10,000, and leaving more than 300,000 homeless.

Amid the tragedy, the Taiwanese received a few bits of unexpected, positive news. Rescue workers found two survivors who had been trapped for five and a half days in their collapsed apartment building in Taipei. Two dogs were rescued in the town of Puli 18 days after the quake.

But one of the most remarkable stories of all occurred on December 9 — more than 11 weeks since the devastating tremor — when a gray and white tabby was discovered alive by workers who were preparing to demolish a damaged house. The family feline, who was long thought to be dead, was pinned under furniture, barely breathing, and severely dehydrated. It weighed less than four pounds—half the weight of a healthy cat its size—and was in a coma and suffering a failing liver.

It had apparently kept itself alive by eating a dead animal because a head, tail, bones, and bits of fur were found next to the survivor. It lapped up rainwater that had seeped through the rubble.

A TV reporter who happened to be on the scene spotted the cat moments before workers would have torn down the house. The reporter took the feline to a veterinary hospital in Taichung, where it was placed in an incubator and fed via a syringe. Later reports indicated the cat recovered and was adopted.

The survival time for people trapped under collapsed buildings varies greatly according to the time of year, terrain, and any physical injuries. One theory says those who aren't rescued within 48 hours have only a 10 percent chance of survival. The odds of a cat being found alive nearly 80 days later are in the billions.

THE TOUGHEST KITTEN

Paddy Paws, an eight-month-old kitten in Carlisle, England, was left for dead by the side of the road after being struck by a car. But the tough-minded cat wasn't ready to die.

Despite two broken hind legs, he crawled home while enduring a week of freezing temperatures.

"When he came through the door dragging his back legs behind him, it was like seeing him come back from the dead," his owner, Gabrielle Stephenson-Bell, told the local newspaper, the *News & Star*.

In January 2010, she had let the cat out, but he didn't return. Stephenson-Bell and her family put up missing posters and searched for Paddy Paws. The family assumed the worst after an arctic blast swept through Carlisle, and Paddy was still missing.

"[We] had started to think about moving on and telling ourselves we wouldn't see him again," recalled Stephenson-Bell.

But seven days later, Paddy Paws found his way home even though he was severely injured. His owner rushed him to the veterinarian, who discovered the kitten had been hit by a car that broke his hind legs and then spent a week in the cold without food. The cat required two operations, including one to insert pins into his fractured limbs.

Stephenson-Bell said the family couldn't afford to pay for the surgery. "But because of the fighting spirit he has shown we were desperate not to have him put down," she said.

The story of Paddy Paws's plight hit the Internet, especially cat lovers' sites, and within days, donations from the United States, Europe, and Australia poured in to cover the costs of the operations. "I have been bowled over by the response we have received," said Stephenson-Bell. "I have e-mailed all the lovely people with kind hearts to thank them for their support." Donations above the cost of the operation were given to the Cats' Protection League.

"He is doing so well," Stephenson-Bell said after the surgeries. "We are all just excited he is back."

STAYIN' ALIVE

A year-old German shepherd was hit by a train and left for dead for a week in the snow—but he made a miraculous recovery.

In 1992, an engineer on the commuter train that runs between South Bend and Michigan City, Indiana, reported that his train had struck and killed a dog. The presumably dead animal lay in a snowbank for a week.

But when another train engineer, Ted Nekvasil, rode past the dog, he was stunned to see the animal was still alive. "He had somehow pushed himself up on his front legs, but his back half wasn't moving," Nekvasil recalled. On his return trip, the engineer stopped his passenger train to check on the dog. He found a weak, bony German shepherd that could barely move. The engineer notified the dispatcher to get help for the dog and offered to pay the costs of the rescue.

Two railroad workers, Bill Reshkin and Steve Pollack, volunteered to comfort the pooch. When they reached him, the injured dog slowly wagged his tail and let them carry him in a blanket. They brought him to an animal clinic in Michigan City, where they were met by Nekvasil and veterinarian Dr. Christine Ellis.

After examining the animal, taking X-rays, and checking blood work, Dr. Ellis found no broken bones or internal injuries. "I still didn't think he had much of a chance of survival," she recalled. "I thought about putting him to sleep. He had been in a coma and lying in the cold for a week and was suffering from hypothermia [loss of body heat]. His muscles had atrophied [wasted away]. But then he lifted his head, looked up at me with those big trusting eyes, and wagged his tail. That's when I thought, 'We can't let him die without giving him a chance.'

"He began eating, and we worked with him every day with his therapy to stretch out his muscles. He was so accepting. He never complained, even though the therapy had to hurt."

Dr. Ellis believed that when struck by the commuter train, the dog had received a glancing blow to the head that left him unconscious. Ironically, lying in the snow and cold probably saved his life, she said. The cold slowed down his body functions, known as metabolism, allowing him to survive for the week. Had it been warm, he probably would have died from dehydration.

Dr. Ellis gave him the name Trainwreck, because every day she would enter the clinic and ask, "How's my train wreck dog?"

It took Trainwreck weeks, but he eventually was able to walk again. After efforts to find his owner proved futile, he was given a new home on a farm near Michigan City.

"He was such a sweet, loving dog," said Dr. Ellis. "He touched all our hearts."

WHERE THERE'S SMOKA, THERE'S FIRE

There's no doubt that Smoka the cat used up most of her nine lives. She endured a raging fire in a three-story-tall building—and survived. When the building collapsed, she rode the flaming second floor to the ground—and survived. She was buried under tons of smoking rubble—and survived. She was doused with thousands of gallons of water from fire hoses — and survived. She was trapped in the debris for nearly a month — and survived. Just when her situation seemingly couldn't get any worse, she lay helplessly in the charred remains as a wrecking crew's heavy equipment rumbled directly above her — and survived.

The one-and-a-half-year-old gray cat was the lovable pet of Sandy LaPierre of Franklin, Ohio. They lived in a second-floor apartment of a building that housed a florist shop. In the early morning hours of August 9, 2009, the structure caught fire.

Dennie Fitzgerald, who owned the shop and lived in the building, immediately woke his tenants, including LaPierre. Terrified by the smoke, Smoka scampered under the bed and refused to come out. LaPierre didn't want to leave her cat behind, but because the smoke and flames were getting worse, Fitzgerald pulled the woman down the stairs. All the tenants escaped safely.

The building burned for six hours and shook from explosions caused by five ruptured gas lines before it collapsed. The fire department used 30,000 gallons of water to finally douse the fire.

Everyone assumed that Smoka had died. "I thought she was gone for sure," LaPierre told the local newspaper the *Middletown Journal.* "There was no way" she could have survived.

Nearly four weeks after the fire, Stark Wrecking Services began clearing away the debris when one of the workers spotted a furry head poking up from beneath 16 feet of rubble.

"I imagine twenty to thirty tons of trash were on top of the cat," said Clarence Witte, who was operating a backhoe. "I figured it was a burnt, dead cat, but I looked out the window and saw the cat's eyes, which were as big as saucers. That backhoe weighs forty thousand pounds, so I don't know why it didn't get squished."

Removing debris carefully by hand, workers dug Smoka out and laid her on top of the rubble. "Its body was stiff," Witte told pawnation.com. "The only thing moving was its head." But the cat, who was thin and weak, eventually tried to get up.

"There's no way to explain how that cat survived in there," said Witte. "That cat had willpower, I guess, and just did not want to die."

Workers phoned Fitzgerald, who had an employee take Smoka away in a pet carrier, then called LaPierre. "I dropped everything when Dennie called and I went down to see her," LaPierre told pawnation.com. "It was incredible. I cried when I saw her. Smoka heard my voice and started meowing."

The cat was her only possession recovered from the fire. "She is a miracle after staying there almost a month in the rubble," said La Pierre.

Smoka was immediately taken to a vet, who found the cat was dehydrated, had a small infection in one eye, and had several cuts and abrasions. She lost a lot of weight and had difficulty walking at first, but otherwise was in good health.

"With those big bulldozers rolling over the top of that thing day after day, [Smoka] should not have made it," said Fitzgerald. "Nine lives or not, this cat had no business being alive."

Inspiring Survivals

THE DOG WHO BEAT DEATH

Few dogs ever had to face death as often as Roadie the coonhound.

The nine-month-old miracle mutt was hit by a train, lay helplessly between the tracks for three days as dozens of trains roared over him, suffered the loss of two legs, and twice faced attempts to shoot him. Yet, incredibly, he survived . . . and thrived.

"He had a heart as big as all outdoors," said Dr. Mike Griffitt, the veterinarian who saved the dog. "He deserved a second chance."

Actually, Roadie avoided death time and time again.

His ordeal began in November 1992, when he was hunting with his owner in the woods near Nicholasville, Kentucky. While chasing a raccoon onto nearby railroad tracks, Roadie was struck by a freight train. His owner, who had lost sight of the dog, searched for Roadie without success.

Despite being hit by a train, Roadie clung to life.

For three days, the bleeding dog lay between the rails, unable to move because his left front leg and right rear leg had been mangled. More than 50 trains passed over him, but he survived because he was laid out flat between the rails.

A railroad worker spotted the critically injured dog and mercifully tried to end his suffering. The man pulled out his pistol and squeezed the trigger, but the gun jammed.

"When the man got home that night, his pistol fired the first time he pulled the trigger," said Dr. Griffitt. "I guess Roadie wasn't meant to die."

The railroad worker summoned the police who, in turn, called Dr. Griffitt, of the Bluegrass Veterinary Clinic. "When I got there, the dog was lying between the tracks with his head on the ground," recalled the vet. "He was the most pitiful sight I've ever seen, and it brought tears to my eyes. Two of his legs were shredded. It was raining and cold. He was gray from the grease, dirt, and soot of the trains passing over him. I've treated animals for fifteen years, but I've never seen anything as sorrowful as that dog."

While most frightened, injured animals snarl, Roadie wagged his tail when Dr. Griffitt approached him. "I thought, 'This dog must have a tremendous will to live,'" said the vet. "He was so happy to see me. There was no way I could put him to sleep after all he'd been through."

Dr. Griffitt gingerly picked up the dog, drove him to the clinic, and called the owner listed on the dog's collar. When the owner arrived, he took one look at Roadie and said he would take the dog home and shoot him to put him out of his misery.

"I put the dog in the guy's truck," recalled Dr. Griffitt. "As I walked away, I turned and looked back at him one more time. The dog looked at me and wagged his tail. That did it. I couldn't let him go."

Dr. Griffitt talked the owner into letting him keep the dog. The first thing the vet did was give the coonhound the name Railroad, or Roadie for short. The next day, Dr. Griffitt amputated the dog's two mangled legs and nursed him back to health. Amazingly, within a week, the pooch was back on his feet—all two of them.

After that, Roadie did most anything he wanted to do—run, play, and leap into someone's lap. He even could jump into the vet's truck.

When the area newspaper, the *Lexington Herald-Leader,* ran a feature about Roadie's incredible ordeal, animal lovers sent cards and letters, and even money.

His story was told in magazines and song and on radio and television. People stopped by the clinic, where he had a bed behind the front counter, just to see him. He touched a lot of lives because he was a symbol of perseverance, especially to people with disabilities.

He lived for a remarkable 14 years, dying of old age in 2006. "Roadie loved everybody," said Dr. Griffitt. "He was happy all the time."

SNOWED UNDER

A mother cat was determined to keep her five kittens alive, even if it meant sacrificing herself in a bitter winter storm. She curled herself around her babies for warmth in a snowbank. But as the snow and temperatures continued to fall, she and the kittens became trapped, because the snowbank froze.

And yet they all lived. But only because of a persistent, nosy dog.

Mike Lalley and his yellow Labrador retriever, Jessie, were walking in open farmland behind their home in Cedarburg, Wisconsin, on a cold January day in 2001. Suddenly, Jessie bounded off, stopped in the middle of a field, and began digging frantically. Lalley whistled repeatedly for her to return, but she refused.

After he walked over to his excited dog, who was

still digging, Lalley saw fur protruding from the frozen snow. Thinking that Jessie had found a dead creature, Lalley nudged it with his toe. He was startled to see a cat raising her head.

Jessie's whimpers turned to barks. Lalley held his dog tightly as he bent down to examine the scene. He realized that the cat was trapped, her fur frozen to the hard-packed snow. He later told the *Milwaukee Journal Sentinel* that he freed the cat from the snow by pounding on the icy crust with his glove. One of the cat's paws was particularly difficult to break free, he said. "Basically, the fur around her body was frozen into the snow. She was stuck."

When he finally got her out, the bedraggled cat was too weak and sick to run away. Looking into the hole of the snowbank, Lalley made an even bigger discovery. Five shivering kittens were inside huddled together. It was obvious that the grown cat had been on top of them, trying to keep them warm.

Figuring they were suffering from hypothermia, Lalley brought the cats to his home and began to warm them in the bathroom. At the same time, Jessie was desperate to make sure her little charges were safe. "She sniffed nonstop at the crack under the door," he said.

"I didn't think the cat that was on top was going to

live. The others slept four or five hours, and then they were running around, kicking up a storm."

When morning came, Lalley brought his recovering feline family to the Ozaukee Humane Society, where the cats snuggled in blankets and heating pads and were given warm food. The humane society determined that the adult cat was the mother of the kittens. Apparently, they were house pets who had been lost or, more likely, abandoned.

"It's truly amazing that they lived," said Jennifer Pierce-Sylvester, executive director of the humane society. The animals were treated at the shelter for exposure and later put up for adoption.

For discovering the homeless feline family, Jessie was honored by the North Shore Animal League America, a Port Washington, New York, organization that gives out a monthly award to a deserving pet. Said league official Kristin von Kreisler, "This inspiring and unusual survival story tells of compassion shown by both dog and cat."

THE PLUCKY PONY

A small, gray-speckled pony named Molly has become an inspiration for people of all ages — especially those who've lost a limb.

It's no wonder. Left abandoned by her owners when deadly Hurricane Katrina slammed into Louisiana in 2005, she survived the storm and the flooding that followed. Then she had to fend for herself for a few weeks until she was rescued and taken to a horse farm. But she soon lost a leg from injuries caused by a vicious attack by a pit bull.

Rather than give up, Molly showed an incredible spirit and will to live, so much so that her caretakers decided against putting her down. She was fitted with an artificial leg — a rarity among horses — and ever since has been a living symbol of courage and hope.

The real-life saga of the 15-year-old pony began when she was found wandering in a pasture in St. Charles Parish two weeks after the hurricane. An animal-rescue group alerted horse-farm owner Kaye Harris to Molly's plight. Harris brought the pony to her farm in St. Rose, Louisiana, to join other abandoned animals, including 17 ponies.

Four months later, Molly was mauled by a pit bull terrier, an adopted animal who apparently was still traumatized by Katrina and its aftermath. The pony suffered severe injuries to her jaw, belly, and all four legs.

"I thought she was going to die of shock before anything else," Harris told the *New York Times*. Dr.

Allison D. Barca, a local horse veterinarian who treated Molly, didn't give the pony much chance of surviving. But Molly proved that despite her sweet disposition, she had an inner strength to live.

During her recovery, an infection destroyed her right front leg, which, in cases like that, meant she would have to be euthanized. However, Harris and Dr. Barca felt Molly deserved another chance. They went to the veterinary hospital at Louisiana State University, trying to persuade the vets to save Molly. Initially the doctors refused. "This [operation] is almost never done," said Dr. Barca, a close friend of Harris's. "It's so expensive and so hard, and everyone who tries fails. But we just asked them to spend some time with Molly."

After observing Molly for a couple of days, Dr. Rustin M. Moore, a veterinary surgeon and the director of the veterinary school's equine health studies program, noticed that the horse possessed an amazing ability to adapt. He saw how the pony was careful to lie down on different sides so she didn't get sores, and how she allowed people to handle her. "Molly protected her injured leg," he said. "She constantly shifted her weight and didn't overload her good leg. She was a smart pony with a serious survival ethic."

Dr. Moore became convinced Molly would be a good candidate for an artificial leg, known as a prosthesis. "She's very intelligent, and she knows how to take care of herself," he added.

The doctors contacted a local company, Bayou Orthotic and Prosthetic Center, to see if it could create a limb for Molly. The company had never made one for an animal, but artificial limb builder Dwayne Mara agreed to try. He watched ponies walk, to see how their joints bent as they moved. He studied horse anatomy, and he calculated how much weight the limb could support.

In January 2006, Dr. Moore and a team of surgeons amputated Molly's leg below the knee and fitted her with a temporary artificial limb. They knew almost immediately after the operation that it had been a success. Molly walked out of the clinic under her own power.

"She went out, and she went right to putting her weight on it, and I just cried because I knew it was going to work," said Harris.

A permanent prosthesis, which the manufacturer didn't charge for, was put on several months later. Fittingly, it sports a smiley-face imprint on the bottom.

"This was the right horse and the right owner," Dr.

Moore said. "Molly happened to be a one-in-a-million patient. She's tough as nails but sweet, and she was willing to cope with pain. She made it obvious she understood that she was in trouble."

Molly doesn't wear the artificial leg all the time. Often she hobbles around on just three legs and lets her caretakers know when she wants to wear it. "She will put her little limb out, and come to you and let you know that she wants you to put it on," said Dr. Barca. "Sometimes she wants you to take it off, too." Once in a while, Molly will play hard to get with the vet. "It can be pretty bad when you can't catch a three-legged horse."

Harris started taking Molly to shelters, hospitals, nursing homes, and rehabilitation centers to inspire and motivate patients and people with disabilities. Children, especially those being fitted for artificial limbs, identify with a horse who wears a metal leg.

"Molly is a fighter," said Harris's daughter, Erin. "Mom has called her a symbol of New Orleans. She shows that despite Hurricane Katrina and having your leg amputated, you can pull through. People see her as an inspiration."

Added Dr. Moore, "It's obvious to me that Molly had a bigger role to play in life. She survived the hurricane, she survived a horrible injury, and now she is giving hope to others."

THE BATTLE AT KRUGER

A young water buffalo had the worst possible day of his life. He was caught in a tug-of-war between some lions and a crocodile—and he was the "rope."

Although it looked like he would soon be dinner for the winner, the little buffalo never gave up and fought back with all his might. Unbelievably, with the help of his fellow buffaloes, he escaped!

His astounding survival was caught on camera and seen around the world, offering hope to the hopeless.

Witnessing the drama firsthand were six tourists on a safari with a guide in the vast Kruger National Park, South Africa, in 2004. Standing by their vehicle across from a large watering hole, they were awestruck by the incredible confrontation between a herd of Cape buffalo, a small pride of lions, and a pair of crocodiles.

It all began when dozens of water buffalo approached the water, unaware that six lions were resting nearby upwind. Seeing an easy meal coming their way, the concealed lions crouched low and waited for their unsuspecting prey to wander closer. Then the lions charged the herd. While the buffalo were fleeing, the fastest lion singled out a young buffalo and tackled him, knocking both into the water.

Within seconds, the other lions joined the fray. The youngster refused to go down easily. Still in the water, he kicked and squirmed as the lions began dragging him out. They used their paws to pull him by the neck and shoulders.

Making his bad day even worse, a pair of huge crocodiles swam over. One of them clamped its jaws on the buffalo's left hind leg and tried to yank him back into the water. The lions were in no mood to give up their catch, so they continued to pull the poor little buffalo up the bank. The croc held on for as long as it could, but it finally let go because it was outnumbered.

It looked like the pride had won the tug-of-war and the young water buffalo had lost his life. But just as the lions were preparing to eat him, the buffalo herd reorganized and moved in on the predators. A large male buffalo charged one of the lions, kicked it, and ran it off. Still intent on eating, the other lions surrounded the little buffalo.

But not for long. As the herd closed in on the pride, another big male buffalo stepped forward, lowered its head, and with its horns, flung a lion into the air. When the lion landed hard on the ground, several buffaloes chased it away. That got the attention of the rest of the lions and emboldened the herd. The buffaloes moved in and began kicking and bullying the remaining lions.

Meanwhile, to the amazement of the tourists who were watching this extraordinary spectacle, the feisty young buffalo jumped to his feet, slipped out of the grasp of the lions, and disappeared into the safety of the herd. The buffaloes then shooed away the rest of the lions.

"These kinds of animals collaborate all the time," said University of Pennsylvania animal behaviorist Sue McDonnell. "The larger herd is broken down into smaller harems, with a dominant male and several females and their babies. If a youngster is threatened, both the harem males and bachelor males—which usually fight with one another—will get together to try to rescue it."

How the young buffalo survived the tug-of-war, no one can say. Perhaps he was even tougher and scrappier than most members of his herd.

"The guide told us that in his fifteen years of doing this, he'd never seen anything like it," American tourist Jason Schlosberg told *Time* magazine.

He took still pictures of the battle while fellow

tourist Dave Budzinski shot the video and put it on YouTube, where it has been a sensation ever since. As of 2011, it has been viewed more than 59 million times.

SNAKEBIT HERO

A golden retricver named Brutis attacked a deadly coral snake that was heading toward two small children. He saved their lives . . . but nearly lost his after the snake bit him.

Brutis's heroism and close brush with death happened in 2003 on a 10-acre ranch in Hudson, Florida, where he lived with his owners, Fran Oreto and her husband, Mark Asbury.

The couple were unpacking a badminton game while their two grandchildren, Angelique, three, and Lucca, two, were playing by the swings. Suddenly, a coral snake—one of America's deadliest snakes—slithered toward them. Seeing they were in danger, the six-year-old dog pounced on the poisonous reptile and then picked it up with his teeth.

The snake was coiling, trying to strike Brutis. Oreto yelled at the dog to release the snake.

"If he hadn't gotten the snake, it could have gotten the kids. It could have gotten me," Oreto told the *St. Petersburg Times*.

Asbury grabbed the 16-inch-long snake, ran inside, and threw it in the freezer. Oreto rifled through a kitchen drawer until she found a snake chart, which showed that the snake with the black head and red and yellow bands was indeed the extremely poisonous coral snake.

Brutis had followed her inside. But when he looked up at her, his eyes were glazed. Then the 107-pound dog slumped to the floor. Oreto knew why: Her loyal dog had been bitten . . . and now the deadly venom was killing him.

Oreto and Asbury put Brutis, who was completely limp, in the front seat of their SUV. Then Oreto sped toward town in a race against time. On the way, Brutis showed signs that he was dying. He had trouble breathing and was vomiting. With one arm on the wheel and the other trying to keep his head up, Oreto pleaded with him to stay alive.

When they reached Animal Emergency of Pasco, vets told Oreto that they could give Brutis something to relax him and ease his suffering, but there was little else they could do. He would likely die within a few hours.

"The vet said, 'Don't get your hopes up,'" recalled Oreto. "'We'll do what we can do.' But I said, 'He can get through this.'"

His only hope—and it was a slim one at best—was to get injected with antivenom, something the clinic didn't have.

Oreto knew that Brutis had a strong will. And he was just too good a dog to let die without trying everything possible. Armed with a phone book and a phone, Oreto tried to buy the precious antivenom, which cost $900 a vial. "I dialed all the local hospitals," she told the paper. "I started praying and calling. Praying and calling."

Coral-snake antivenom was in short supply and used almost exclusively for humans. Hospitals that had it needed to maintain at least five vials. The first six hospitals Oreto called didn't have any that they could sell her. But the seventh, Morton Plant North Bay Hospital in New Port Richey, had seven, of which two were ready to expire. Oreto sent a friend, Molly Jamison, to pick up a vial.

It had been three hours since Brutis had been bitten, and he was fading fast. Neurotoxins—poisons in the venom that destroy nerve cells—were spreading through his body, and his red blood cell count was falling, which meant that not enough oxygen was getting to the tissues. The vets kept pumping Brutis full of steroids to stabilize him.

Jamison returned a half hour later with the antivenom, which was slowly injected into the dog. When the process was over, Oreto sat on the floor with Brutis. "I didn't want him to think he was being punished or abandoned," she told the newspaper.

At 11:30 P.M., about eight hours after he was brought to the animal clinic, Brutis appeared stable, so Oreto went home. But she received a call from the vets 90 minutes later that the dog's condition had worsened. They would need more antivenom. Oreto sped to the hospital and returned to the vets with the second vial.

Brutis was barely hanging on. After the antivenom treatments and a blood transfusion, he slowly began to improve. As a treat, Oreto brought him his favorite hamburger rolls and, on the following day, an oven-roasted lemon-pepper chicken.

After several days, Brutis was finally allowed to go home. It took another three months before he recovered, although he walked with a limp and tired easily. "The doctors were constantly astonished by his progress," Oreto said. "It's quite an amazing feat that he survived at all. He was a strong enough dog to pull through."

Even though the vet bills totaled $5,000, Oreto said she would do it again. "He's a family member."

And a recognized hero, too. In 2004, Brutis was given the National Dog Hero award by the SPCA (Society for the Prevention of Cruelty to Animals) in Los Angeles. Said chapter president Madeline Bernstein, "A lot of dogs might have just barked or run away. But Brutis went for the snake and took the bite."

Toughing It Out

WILDERNESS CAT

Fluffy, a spoiled, long-haired housecat who loved to be cuddled, wound up fending for herself in the wilds of Montana for three harrowing months. Surprisingly, the cat showed that she possessed the necessary survival skills to avoid becoming dinner for the thousands of predators that roamed the area.

Her life in the wilderness was a far cry from her days in Houston, Texas, where she lived with Philip Wattenbarger; his wife, Elizabeth Ayers; and their three little girls, six-year-old twins Tamara and Evelyn and eight-year-old Marisa, who liked to dress Fluffy in doll clothes and carry her to their tea parties. "She loves to be held like a baby," said Ayers. "She snuggles down and purrs."

In summer 2008, the family took Fluffy and their other cat Tiger—who were both adopted from the pound a year earlier—with them on a camping trip to Yellowstone National Park. While at a West Yellowstone campground, the family allowed the cats to walk around the campsite. Although Tiger stayed nearby, Fluffy disappeared.

For days, the family scoured the brush and peered up at treetops in a panicked search for their beloved pet. The family's three children were understandably in tears about losing their cat. "Tamara in particular had been very upset," Ayers told the local newspaper, the *Bozeman Daily Chronicle.* "Every day she'd say, 'Mom, is Fluffy coming back?'"

Wattenbarger and Ayers figured that the cat had been caught, killed, and eaten by a coyote, wolf, fox, owl, eagle, bobcat, grizzly bear, or some other predator. Although Ayers was sure that Fluffy was dead, she couldn't bring herself to tell that to her children.

What the family didn't know was that Fluffy was indeed alive, and finding ways to steer clear of the many predators that would have loved to snack on a little housecat. She kept her belly full by catching birds and chipmunks. She even found shelter in a neighbor's garage by slipping in and out of a small hole in the door, caused when bears had broken in months earlier.

At the end of summer, neighbors at Horse Butte, about a mile from the campground, noticed a stray cat and started leaving food for what turned out to be Fluffy. Although she was wearing a harness with a tag, she was so skittish that no one could get close enough to catch her and read the tag.

With winter approaching, Norval and Shirley Armstrong felt an obligation to save her, so they borrowed a live trap and successfully captured the cat. Their son, Rick Armstrong, picked up the trap, brought it in the house, and read her tag, which listed her owners' phone number.

"Five minutes later, my mother called the people in Houston," Armstrong told the paper. "They couldn't believe it."

Ayers admitted, "We were sure she was coyote bait. She wasn't the smarter of our two cats, so we were quite surprised. She had more skills than we expected."

Minutes after she was caught, Fluffy began rubbing up against her rescuers and purring up a storm. Armstrong said she was "very, very hungry." They took her to a vet, who said she was in excellent condition, considering what she had been through.

Neighbor Anne Kinney, a retired Delta Airlines flight attendant who could fly for free, escorted Fluffy on a flight to Houston. When the cat was let out of her carrier, the girls mobbed her. "We were all thrilled when she got home," said Ayers, who paid the cat's vet bill and fee for allowing Fluffy to fly in the plane's cabin.

Despite her misadventure, Fluffy still joins the family on their camping trips. But she never strays far from the campsite.

A BEAR OF A DOG

For three and a half years, Lucas, a hound dog from South Carolina, was lost in the brutal Canadian wilderness and given up for dead, presumably fatally mauled by a bear.

But then one day, long after his owner had lost hope of ever seeing the dog again, Lucas was found alive—scrawny and shy, but very much alive.

His saga began in fall 1988, when he and his owner, Earl Cash, a self-employed contractor and Baptist minister in Pickens, South Carolina, were on a hunting trip in the backwoods near Sudbury, Ontario. The hound spotted a black bear and chased him deep into the forest. Cash lost sight of the dog, but minutes later, he heard Lucas yelp in pain. "I heard him holler, and I knew the bear had hit him or bit him," said Cash.

The owner spent the next five days scouring the woods in search of his prized dog. But he finally gave up and headed home without the pooch. The next year, Cash returned to the area and looked for his dog again. "I asked people if they had seen a black and tan hound," he recalled. "I got no results, so I just gave him up for dead."

Then, in February 1992 — three and a half years after he last saw Lucas — Cash received a phone call that left him thunderstruck. The call was from Jane Neve, an animal-control officer from Rayside-Balfour, Ontario. She told Cash she had a hound in her pound with a license tag that identified the canine as Lucas.

"I said, 'Say what?'" recalled Cash. "And then she said he was a black and tan hound, and I knew she had my dog. I was very surprised, I guarantee you. I was speechless. I had given up all hope of ever seeing Lucas again. I just couldn't believe it."

For over a year before he was caught, Lucas would wander into the town, but never let people get too close to him. Lucas, whom residents nicknamed the Phantom, would forage through garbage cans for food and then scoot off into the woods, only to return days or even weeks later. He was allowed to roam around town because he never bothered anyone.

But eventually, Neve felt it was best to catch him. She nabbed him when he fell asleep after eating canned cat food laced with a tranquilizer. Neve then brought Lucas to the animal shelter, where she gave him a checkup. Other than being about ten pounds underweight, the dog was remarkably healthy.

Using the information on the dog's tag, Neve contacted Cash with the astonishing news.

"It's amazing that Lucas survived as he did, because we often get temperatures as low as minus fifteen degrees up here," Neve told reporters. "In the summer, the mosquitoes are so bad even the moose come out of the bush to get into the wind."

A month after he was captured, Lucas, accompanied by Neve, flew back home to South Carolina on a trip paid for by the *Sudbury Star* newspaper. At the Greenville-Spartanburg Airport, Lucas arrived to a hero's welcome.

"You rascal, you," Cash said, giving him a big hug after attaching a yellow ribbon to the dog's collar. Lucas remained quiet at first, somewhat scared by all the attention. But within a matter of minutes, he perked up and nuzzled his owner.

"He recognized me," said Cash, beaming with joy. "I'm just so glad to have him back."

(NEAR) DEATH TRAP

Sheba the Siberian husky was caught in a hunter's steel trap for nearly two excruciating weeks in bitter subzero cold, yet she survived.

Sheba lived with workers for a natural-gas company in a remote camp 320 miles north of Edmonton, Alberta, Canada. One morning in 1991, while on an outing with a worker, she darted off into the woods, chasing a small animal. During her pursuit, she stepped into a trap, and the steel jaws snapped shut on her right front paw. When Sheba didn't return, workers searched the woods for her, but to no avail.

"The crew thought she must have been killed by a bear," said Jerome Tangedal, a company supervisor.

Sheba was alive, but fading. No matter how hard she struggled, she couldn't free herself from the trap's deadly jaws. Day after day, she grew weaker from hunger, pain, and the bone-numbing cold. But she didn't give up. She stayed alive by licking the snow and fending off wolves with her growls and barks.

Finally, 13 long days after the trap had snared her, Sheba was found by gas worker Worley Rosson. He had gone out with another dog to check on a gas meter when his pooch began to bark. "Then I heard Sheba reply in a tiny, low whine," recalled Rosson. "I went rushing through the dense brush, and there she was, about a quarter mile away with her paw caught in a trap."

Rosson pried open the trap and brought Sheba back to the camp, where he warmed her and fed the famished dog all the food her stomach could hold. The dog had dropped in weight from 120 pounds down to 90. Unfortunately, gangrene had set in her wounded leg and a few days later, her limb was amputated.

A dog lover who had learned about her ordeal carved a wooden peg and attached it to her stump with a bracket and two Velcro straps. Sheba adjusted to her artificial limb and was back trekking in the woods with her loving workers.

Said Tangedal, "Sheba had a heart as big as the great outdoors."

DOGGED DETERMINATION

Buck was a seven-year-old golden retriever spoiled by his loving family, who let him have the run of the house. But after getting lost during a family trip far from home, the pampered pooch somehow managed to survive five harsh months alone in the frigid winter wilderness of Montana before he was found.

Kimberly and Chuck Halter, of Bonney Lake, Washington, along with their sons, Jason and Josh, and the family dog were on a road trip to see an ailing relative in Montana in August 2008. At a rest stop in Chester, Montana, everyone piled out of the car. Buck was not on a leash because he was an obedient dog that always stayed close to Jason, 17.

As luck would have it, a freight train let loose with a loud whistle as it rattled across the railroad trestle that spanned the rest area. "When Buck heard the whistle, he took off like a shot," Halter told the Associated Press. "None of us even saw him."

Maxine Woods, who lived across the highway, waved her arms and shouted to the Halters that she saw their dog run off and disappear. The Halters drove around the small town, looking for Buck. Woods joined in the search. "She got in her car, started calling people, and before you knew it, everybody around there was looking for our dog," Halter said.

"We went to the library, and the librarian in Chester made us posters and wouldn't charge us a dime for them." The family put up posters in banks and post offices in small towns around the area. The Halters pinned flyers on posts along roads stretching 40 miles in each direction, hoping someone would spot their cherished pet. "That was about all we could do."

After two days of searching, no one had seen Buck. The Halters even slept in their car during those two nights, hoping he'd find his way back. The brokenhearted family finally left Chester to visit their relative. On their return home, they stopped again in the town, but no one had seen Buck.

As fall turned into winter, heavy snow covered the Chester area, and temperatures occasionally fell to 20 below zero. "Every time we'd hear about the weather, we would just cringe," Halter recalled. "I would cry even harder, thinking, 'Where is my Buck?' And of course I couldn't let my son Jason know. I never let him see me cry, because he kept the faith and kept the hope. He would tell me all the time that Buck's coming home. He actually thought he was going to walk home like in [the movie] *Homeward Bound*."

Friends and relatives told Halter there was no way Buck could survive a Montana winter in the wilderness, especially with wolves and coyotes roaming the area.

More than five months after Buck ran off, on a day when the temperature plunged to 27 degrees below zero, Jason Wanken first saw a stray golden retriever on his family farm just north of Chester. After spotting the pooch over the next several days, Wanken used a snowmobile to bring food to the dog, who had taken up residence under a collapsed barn.

Meanwhile, Wanken's mother remembered the name of the golden retriever that went missing the previous summer. She suggested that the next time

Wanken saw the dog, he call him Buck. "The next day, I took the boys out with me, and I had a full bag of food with me, and I just rattled that bag," Wanken later told the Associated Press. "I started to feed [the dog] and could actually pet it then."

Eventually they used food to lure the dog into a cage. "I thought it couldn't be the same dog [that was missing], because it had been too long," Wanken said.

Just to be sure, they brought the dog over to Maxine Woods's house. Woods thought there was a chance the pooch was indeed the missing Buck. With the number she got off the "Lost Dog" poster, she phoned Kim Halter and took photos of the dog.

"She e-mailed me three pictures, and when I was on the phone with her I received the pictures," Halter recalled. "I said that was him, and we both started crying."

The Halters drove 750 miles in 16 hours, through the night, to Chester. "When we got to the Wankens, Buck ran right up to us, and it was absolutely without a doubt him," Halter said. "He looked at us and we looked at him, and we were all crying. It was beyond amazing."

The dog, who had weighed 110 pounds before he went missing, had lost about 40 pounds but was otherwise in good condition. When the Halters brought him home, his veterinarian confirmed the dog definitely was Buck, not that the family needed any proof. The Halters then outfitted him with new tags, a microchip, a well-fitting collar, and a leash.

"His first night back home, Buck climbed into bed and went to sleep, like old times, and slept so soundly he was snoring," Halter said. "We don't know what he had to do to survive, but now he could finally really relax and rest."

THE GOLDEN GHOST

Sam the runaway golden retriever survived two bitter New England winters, wild animals, hunters, and hunger. He dodged his owners, dog lovers, and animal-control officers who looked for him. Even helicopter searches couldn't find him.

His skills at survival and vanishing without a trace were so sharp that they earned him the nickname the Golden Ghost.

After two years on the run, Sam was finally captured with the help of a ham dinner, a surveillance camera, and a remote-controlled net.

Peg and Dennis Sklarski, of Deerfield, New Hampshire, adopted Sam in 2004, after he was rescued from an abused life in Tennessee. Because the two-year-old dog had been mistreated there, he didn't trust humans. Three weeks after the couple brought him home, Sam broke from his leash and ran away.

Over the next two years, he roamed the woods, surviving by relying on his keen instincts, picking through garbage cans, and eating food left out by concerned residents. He was spotted in at least six towns by residents who called the Sklarskis with the latest sightings. The couple spent countless hours cruising the area roads for their elusive pet.

Sheriff's deputies and volunteer search parties kept looking for Sam, but whenever he was spotted, he would simply vanish—a trait that turned him into a local legend.

Searchers set up feeding stations and humane traps throughout Rockingham County, not only to make sure the dog had food but also to track his movements in the hope of nabbing him.

"He was a smart dog," Raymond (New Hampshire) Police Department's animal-control officer Tona McCarthy told the *Exeter News-Letter*. "He was eluding professionals. There was no pattern to follow. I kept a log of where he showed up, and he changed his eating time of day from the afternoon to midnight.

We couldn't track his pattern. It was like he knew we were watching him."

During his time on the loose, Sam came close to capture a few times. Steve Sprowl, an investigator with the New Hampshire Society for the Prevention of Cruelty to Animals, tried on several occasions to shoot the dog with a tranquilizer dart, but that didn't work. One attempt at tranquilizing Sam in the winter failed because the sedative in the dart froze.

"It touched my heart to have this two-year-old dog from an abusive/neglect situation," Sprowl told the newspaper. "The Sklarskis spent money and brought him back to New Hampshire. I wanted to invest the time to bring the dog back to them so he knew what it was like to have a loving family."

Sam avoided capture until spring 2006. With the help of donations, the local SPCA bought a remote-controlled net. Along with a surveillance camera, the net was set up on a wooded lot in Raymond, where Helen and Robert Mitchell had been leaving a bowl of food out for Sam. Volunteers watched the camera's monitor from the Mitchells' garage, hoping to release the net over the dog when he tried to eat from the bowl.

After five weeks, McCarthy, who had devoted

hours of his own time trying to catch Sam, spotted the dog in the area. Sam still had on the red harness that he had been wearing the day he ran away in 2004.

The officer went to the Mitchells' garage and watched for Sam on the video monitor. Soon, the dog appeared and cautiously sniffed the air and the ground and looked from side to side. He crept toward a bowl of cooked ham. As Sam gobbled a few mouthfuls, McCarthy hit a switch that released the net and snared him.

Sam was taken to the SPCA in Stratham, where he was treated for Lyme disease and heartworm disease.

Recalled Peg Sklarski, "The first time I saw Sam after he was rescued, I went to his cage and I got down on all fours and said, 'Oh, Sammy boy,' and he looked up at me, and he wagged his tail and he reached his paw out to me."

Sam made a full recovery and was reunited with the Sklarskis. He eventually adjusted to life with caring humans.

"Animals need people to love and survive," McCarthy said. "They depend on us to care for them. This was an animal that had a terrible history with a prior owner. My deal was I had to help this animal. I will never forget this dog."

THE CANINE CASTAWAY

An Australian cattle dog raised as a homebody turned into a canine version of Robinson Crusoe after she ended up a castaway on a deserted island for four months.

Before her ordeal, Sophie Tucker, who was named after a famous singer, was quite content to lie about in air-conditioned comfort in the home of her owners, Jan and David Griffith, of Mackay, Queensland, Australia. But she did enjoy going out on sailing excursions with them on their yacht.

During one such voyage in 2009, the four-year-old dog slipped overboard in choppy seas about 20 miles off the coast of Mackay. "We hit a rough patch and when we turned around, the dog was gone," Jan Griffith told the BBC. "We were able to backtrack to look for her, but because it was a gray day, we just couldn't find her. We thought that once she had hit the water, she would have been gone because the wake from the boat was so big."

Devastated by their failure to find Sophie, the Griffiths returned home heartbroken. What they didn't know was that the dog had survived the plunge and swum nearly six miles in stormy, shark-infested waters to uninhabited St. Bees Island.

For the next four months, the plucky dog lived off the land, eating dead crabs and hunting down smaller animals.

Three rangers on the remote island occasionally spotted a dog they assumed was wild. Sophie had become vicious and wouldn't let anyone go near her, even when the rangers offered her food.

They eventually caught Sophie using a cage and dog food as bait. That's when they realized the dog had been someone's pet.

"The day Sophie was trapped she was nervous, because she had been separated from human contact for a long time, but after a while she settled down," Steve Fisher, ranger in charge, told the local newspaper the *Daily Mercury*.

Griffith never thought she would see her much-loved pet again. But then a friend of the family heard a report about the dog that had been captured on the island. Wondering if by some miracle it was Sophie, Griffith contacted Queensland Parks and Wildlife rangers, who agreed to bring the dog to the mainland.

The rangers noticed a difference in Sophie's mood as their boat neared the town of Mackay where the Griffiths were waiting.

"She was apparently a little vicious when she was

trapped, but when she saw us, she started whimpering and banging the cage," Jan Griffith said. "When they let her out, she just about flattened us."

Vicki Lomax, a Royal SPCA vet, said Sophie's breed and fitness were big factors in her amazing survival. "Cattle dogs are probably the most suited type of dog to survive something like this, but it would have been a major ordeal for her," Dr. Lomax told the *Brisbane Times*. "Five nautical miles is an incredibly big distance to swim for any type of dog. She was lucky she hadn't been taken by a shark. If this had been a smaller dog, I don't think it would have been a happy ending."

Since her rescue, Sophie was quick to readjust to the comforts of home. "She surprised us all," said Jan Griffith. "She was a house dog, and look what she did all on her own."

Do or Die

THE HOGS THAT SAVED THEIR BACON

Two pigs boldly escaped from the slaughterhouse and remained on the run for a week, kindling the compassion of an entire country.

Their breakout led not only to their survival but also a movie about their exploits.

The five-month-old Tamworth pigs, worth about $100 each at market, were sent in a truck to a slaughterhouse in Malmesbury, Wiltshire, England, in 1998. As the pigs were being unloaded, the rebellious pair bolted. They squeezed through a hole in a fence, leaped into the wide, icy River Avon, and swam to freedom on the other side.

As slaughterhouse workers, police, and tracking dogs searched high and low for them, the resourceful pigs avoided capture for days, attracting tremendous media attention and winning the hearts and minds of the animal-loving nation. The runaway porkers were given the names Butch Cassidy and the Sundance Pig.

Even a local butcher expressed the widespread

opinion that it would be "unsporting" to kill the two after such a daring escape.

Geoff Francis, from Hillside Animal Sanctuary near King's Lynn, Norfolk, said he would willingly give the heroic pigs a home for life. "We would love to have this pair," he said. "We already have a refugee from the slaughterhouse, a bullock we called Braveheart, who swam a river to escape—just like the pigs.

"We have been inundated with calls from people asking us to save them. Some have offered money to help us. It is amazing how fugitives like these two catch people's imaginations."

Of the nearly 100 reporters who covered the story, many were from foreign media organizations. NBC sent a film crew with London-based reporter Donatella Lorch, who did a report for *NBC Nightly News*.

The 110-pound pigs outwitted their pursuers with the help of local residents who fed them table scraps. The friends of Butch and Sundance refused to reveal where the pigs were hiding until a local newspaper, the *Daily Mail*, promised to purchase them and send them to an animal sanctuary.

The newspaper bought the pigs from their owner for an undisclosed fee—reportedly several thousands of dollars—in order to have exclusive photo rights.

Only then did a resident tip off authorities to the runaways' location. Handlers hired by the newspaper captured Butch, who turned out to be a sow (female pig). She had been resting in the two-acre backyard of a sympathetic couple who lived less than a mile from the slaughterhouse.

Sundance was much tougher to catch. It took another day and a half to nab him. Two Springer spaniels were needed to flush him out of a dense thicket before a trained marksman fired several tranquilizer darts to bring him down. Sundance was later taken to a nearby animal clinic, where he was examined and declared healthy.

"He is a little bit shaky, but doesn't appear to be any the worse for it," veterinarian Fran Baird said at the time. "I am quite confident he will make a full recovery." Baird added that he had taken precautions to ensure Sundance didn't escape again. "There are padlocks on the doors, which are more than six feet high and chained together. He's obviously quite bright. He's outfoxed a number of people for a number of days."

The pigs were sent to the Rare Breeds Centre, near Ashford, Kent, to live out their natural lives. Meanwhile, the BBC produced a 60-minute film celebrating their escape, called *The Legend of the*

Tamworth Two. Executive producer Sally Woodward told BBC News Online that the film tells how Butch and Sundance became legends and how "the British once again took the underdog—or in this instance, the under-pig—to their hearts and in the process briefly made them the most famous fugitives in the world."

An enormous, 800-pound female hog from Nebraska was riding in a trailer truck with about 90 other pigs, all bound for the slaughterhouse. But when opportunity knocked, she was clever enough to escape.

The truck was rolling through North Little Rock, Arkansas, in 2009 on Interstate 430 when it flipped over, splitting open the trailer and allowing 60 surviving hogs to flee. Police, emergency workers, and volunteers managed to round up all the loose pigs . . . or at least they thought they did.

One, later nicknamed "Ham on the Lam," slipped away and enjoyed freedom in the semirural area for an entire week without being detected. She might have remained hidden longer if it hadn't been for her love of water.

Seven days after the accident, LeAnn Baldy, whose home was near the scene of the accident, was looking out her kitchen window when she noticed that her pool was overflowing. She went outside to investigate and was astounded to see a huge pig wading in the shallow end, slurping water.

"It was crazy, really crazy," Baldy told the *Arkansas Democrat-Gazette*. "I was just shocked. But it's cool. Not many people look out their back window and see a pig in their pool."

Baldy and her husband, Terry, quickly became attached to the porker and nicknamed her Wilburette, after the famous pig in the classic tale *Charlotte's Web*.

Informed by reporters that the animal would likely be taken to its original destination—the sausage factory—LeAnn Baldy asked, "Why can't we call the governor and have him pardon the pig?"

Because the pig had not been convicted of anything, Governor Mike Beebe didn't have any power to offer the hog clemency. But that didn't stop animal lovers from calling the governor, begging him to do something to save the hog.

Meanwhile Baldy kept pleading publicly for a pardon for her uninvited guest, who was still enjoying the refreshing pool. "The pig has made it through a wreck and been all scraped up and made it through all that," she said. "I just don't want it to die."

Baldy's efforts paid off. Jim Stonehocker, executive vice president of the pig's owner, Odom's Tennessee Pride, announced that this particular hog could no longer be used for any of the company's sausage products. "For a week it has been in the wild," he told the press. "What has happened to it? What has it been in contact with? You need to know what your hog has been eating. We believe this hog has earned the right to go and do something else," other than end up on someone's breakfast table.

So Wilburette's life was spared. After getting medical care from the Pulaski County Humane Society, she was sent to live out the rest of her days on a rescue farm in Jefferson County.

CALLING FOR HELP

When Tipper, a nine-month-old cat from Tampa, Florida, was in desperate need of emergency help, he did what we humans would do — called 9-1-1.

Tipper was home alone when he came within a whisker of losing one of his nine lives in 1996. "He got his flea collar stuck in his mouth and started choking," said his owner, Gail Curtis. "He panicked and apparently was racing around the room."

Somehow, the frantic feline knocked the bedroom

phone off the hook and, luckily, stepped on the speed-dial button that Curtis had set to 9-1-1.

"I happened to be cruising in the neighborhood when dispatch told me they had received a nine-one-one call and that no one was on the other line," Deputy Joe Bamford told the *Tampa Tribune.* "I rushed over to the house and broke in. That's when I found the cat gagging and going crazy. I found a handyman next door to help me. We grabbed the cat and wrapped Tipper in a towel, and, with the handyman's help, I removed the collar."

Said Curtis, "I was so relieved that Tipper survived. Thank goodness he was smart enough — well, actually, lucky enough — to dial 9-1-1."

CAT FISH

A cat that had been abandoned on a storm-ravaged ship survived alone at sea for three weeks by catching and eating flying fish.

The feline was a mouser aboard the Norwegian sailing vessel *Birgette* when the ship was battered in a severe storm in the north Atlantic in February 1895. Towering waves toppled the main mast and destroyed the rudder. All the sails had been ripped or blown away.

When the seas calmed down, the rudderless *Birgette*

drifted aimlessly. On February 21, the crew abandoned ship and was taken aboard the Philadelphia-bound steamship *Snowflake*. For whatever reason, the cat was left behind.

Twenty-one days later, on March 12, crewmen aboard the steamer *Potomac*, which was three days out of London, spotted the disabled *Birgette* and sent a party of five sailors to board her. Not finding anyone, they were about to return to their ship when First Officer Dogbein discovered a bony cat peering over the edge of the crow's nest on the mast that wasn't broken.

The officer wanted to reach the cat, but none of the rigging was still standing, and no one cared to climb the mast. "He was about to leave the cat to her fate, when a few gently whispered meows smote upon his ear and awakened memories of home," said a news dispatch dated March 24, 1895. "He decided to have the cat or never again board the *Potomac*. He called for volunteers to save its life."

They threw a line over the gaff—a spar that extended out from the mast—and one of the sailors was pulled up near the crow's nest, but the cat hissed and swiped at him and cowered out of his reach. When the sailor was lowered to the deck, he told the others what he had seen in the crow's nest.

"He said that the cat was surrounded with bones from fish that she had eaten," according to the dispatch. Apparently, she would swat flying fish that vaulted onto the deck and then she would climb up the mast and eat them in the crow's nest. She stayed hydrated by drinking puddles of rainwater.

A second attempt to rescue the cat proved successful. With a flying fish that she had recently caught still in her mouth, the cat was brought safely down to the deck. "It looked the men over, and, still holding the fish, went to the man who had thrown the line, rubbed against his leg, and purred its thanks," said the report. "It was a poor-looking specimen of a cat, but it was taken on board the *Potomac*."

The cat became a loving mascot for her new crewmates. Said the dispatch, "Captain Leitch of the *Potomac* declares that the cat has been entered on the ship's articles as one of the crew, and nothing can get it from his possession."

NO NEED FOR AN APPOINTMENT

A dying sea turtle found a clever way to save itself—by swimming to the world's only medical facility devoted solely to helping sea turtles.

It happened in 2009 when a seriously ill loggerhead turtle swam to Turtle Hospital in Marathon, Florida. Staffers there normally have to go out in the waters off the Florida Keys to find distressed sea turtles and bring them back for treatment. But in this case, the loggerhead swam to within ten feet of the hospital's dock.

Executive director Ryan Butts was the first person to spot the ailing loggerhead in the water behind the facility. "It's very rare to see a turtle in a bay like this," he said in a story for zootoo.com. "I've never actually seen one here [in the water] before."

The turtle showed obvious signs that it was sick. "It had a heavy cover of barnacles on its shell," said Butts. "It looked very, very thin around the neck and shoulder region. For a reptile, that indicates it was sick in some way."

The 72-pound turtle was hoisted out of the water and given a thorough examination, which revealed that it was suffering from a bacterial infection in its bloodstream. The loggerhead would require many weeks of treatment at Turtle Hospital. Bonding immediately with their patient, the staff decided to call it Kincaid.

There was a genuine concern that Kincaid wouldn't survive. But after a week of intensive care in a special water tank, the turtle began to show signs of improvement. Following a regimen of antibiotics and vitamins with a diet of raw squid, Kincaid soon was eating well and responding to the treatment.

Hospital veterinarians couldn't tell if Kincaid was male or female, because the turtle was estimated to be no more than 15 years old. Sea turtles, some of which live to be up to 100 years old, don't reach maturity until their 30s.

This federally protected endangered species is known for its large head and powerful jaws, which allow it to feed on hard-shelled prey such as conch. The species also feeds on fish, crustaceans, and other mollusks and marine animals. An adult grows to an average weight of about 200 pounds. The top shell is slightly heart-shaped with a reddish-brown color.

Turtle Hospital typically treats sea turtles that suffer illness, complications from eating junk carelessly tossed into the ocean, and injuries from boating accidents and from getting their flippers tangled up in fishing lines. "The biggest problem would be boat hits followed by eating garbage like plastic grocery bags and cigarette butts," Butts explained. "That can be absolutely the worst thing for the turtles. It kills thousands a year."

Usually local fishermen and boaters will spot an ailing sea turtle and either get permission to catch it and bring it to the hospital or call staffers to pick it up. But never has a sea turtle just shown up at Turtle Hospital's back door for a walk-in . . . or, in this case, a swim-in appointment.

The hospital, which opened in 1986, had successfully treated and released more than 1,000 turtles. "Our success rate is pretty good," rehab specialist Shane Catts said. "They really are able to recover and do well by themselves" when they go back to the ocean.

After treating Kincaid for nearly ten weeks, staffers decided that the turtle was getting fat and was ready to return to the wild. They arranged for a going-away celebration, inviting the public and TV news crews to watch the turtle's release at a seaside park. Butts said that if Kincaid had not shown up at the hospital on its own, the turtle would have died.

LOCK DOWN

Two bull elk that were fighting each other locked horns so tightly they remained stuck for more than a week. Because the two enemies couldn't separate themselves, they were forced to be nice to each other in order to survive.

When a rancher in Indian Valley, Nevada, spotted the two entangled elk in 2006, he reported them to the local authorities. "[The authorities] were up there the next day and couldn't find the elk," said Nevada Department of Wildlife (NDOW) biologist Tom Donham. "They assumed they must have separated by themselves and didn't think any more about it."

A week later, the rancher was again in Indian Valley searching for some of his cows when he saw the two elk still stuck together. This time he called NDOW. Donham game warden Brian Eller and Bureau of Land Management wildlife biologist Bryson Code drove out to help the animals.

"When we arrived where the rancher had last seen them, we found them pretty quickly," Donham told the local newspaper *The Ely Times*. "They were both lying on the ground, and one of them was in a very uncomfortable . . . position with his head directly above the other's head and his nose pointing straight up to the sky."

Recalled Eller, "Once we found out they were alive, I was hoping they couldn't move and would stay where they were. That didn't happen. When they ran off, I was hoping that they couldn't go very far. That didn't happen, either."

Although the elk might have been enemies at the start of their fight, they used teamwork to run for nearly a mile to evade the three men. "As [we] approached, they both got to their feet and ran down the canyon while locked together like they had been doing it all their lives," said Donham. "[It was] serious cooperation if I've ever seen it."

After two unsuccessful attempts, Donham shot a tranquilizer dart into one of the elk. With one down, the other elk couldn't run, so it was easy for Donham to tranquilize him, too. When the men tried to separate the two, they discovered the cold weather had blunted the effects of the tranquilizer that was shot into the second elk, and he began to put up a fuss. While Eller and Code held the elk down, Donham painlessly sawed an antler off the other bull with a handsaw.

"As soon as they were apart, the bull that hadn't gotten a full dose jumped to his feet, and [we] quickly gave him all the room he wanted," said Donham. "He went off about thirty yards and lay down for about ten minutes before finally walking up the hill and over the ridge, none the worse for wear."

The men treated the other elk with antibiotics and then watched as it walked away after the tranquilizer wore off.

"If these two bulls had not been discovered, and we never got the call, they more than likely would have both died," said Donham. "Watching the bulls walk away, and knowing that we likely saved them from a slow death was definitely one of those moments that makes this job rewarding."

A SKY-HIGH DOG FIGHT

Ava, a four-year-old dachshund, was plucked out of her yard and carried off by a large bald eagle. But even though the long pooch comes from a breed known as a "wiener dog," she had no intention of being the big bird's next meal.

In an intense, midair struggle, Ava bit the eagle in the leg and freed herself from the clutches of the predator. That was the good news. The bad news was that Ava then plummeted 40 feet to the ground. Fortunately, she survived the fall.

Ava's owner, Jon Martin, of Madison, Maine, typically let her out for her morning routine, which included walking about 500 feet to the home of his son, Jon Martin Jr., so she could play with Jon Jr.'s daughters, ages three and five.

In fall 2001, the father and son began noticing

an eagle flying over the Kennebec River north of downtown Madison. "He always hunts in this area, constantly circling around, way up high," Jon Jr. told the local newspaper the *Kennebec Journal* at the time. "It's a really huge, huge bird. It's really beautiful.

"I told my father, 'Dad, you want to watch out for that eagle. Ava is a little hot dog. That eagle is going to get the dog.' Sure enough, he got the dog."

It happened on a March morning in 2002. Minutes after Ava was let out of the house, the bald eagle swooped out of the sky, clutched the 13-pound dog in its sharp talons, and flew off.

When Jon Sr. realized what had happened, he began running toward the bird, waving his arms and yelling. The eagle had already lifted off the ground and was circling skyward, gripping its prey. But Ava was no patsy. She fought back, twisting and wriggling in a life-and-death struggle to get free. "Then the dog bit him in the leg, so he let her go," Jon Sr. told the paper.

The dog dropped 40 feet and hit the ground hard about 300 feet from where she was snatched. She was seriously injured, but still alive. "The bird's claws had pierced her like a razor," said Jon Jr. "They went right through her body to the other side. She came home bleeding everywhere."

Jon Sr. and his wife, Laura, rushed Ava to the Animal Medical Clinic in nearby Skowhegan, where veterinarian Gail Gibson performed surgery on the dog, whose hind quarters were badly damaged. The operation was a success, and Ava eventually recovered.

As for the bald eagle, Jon Sr. admitted that he was so upset that he wanted to shoot it. But he knew that he couldn't, because although the symbol of America is no longer on the endangered species list, it is still protected by federal law.

Ever since the incident, someone always escorted Ava outside, preventing the eagle from getting another chance to eat a wiener dog.

SEE YA LATER, ALLIGATOR

Tigre the pit bull escaped from the jaws of death—literally. He fought off an alligator that wanted him for breakfast.

His owner, Oscar Alarcon, was walking the two-year-old dog on a leash along the shore of Lake Hunter in Lakeland, Florida, in 2010, as they had done most mornings. Alarcon had seen alligators in the lake during his daily walks, but they were all small, so he wasn't concerned when he let go of the leash and let Tigre wade in to cool off.

Suddenly, a six-foot gator surfaced, lunged for Tigre, and clamped its teeth around his 66-pound body. Then it tried to drag him under the water.

But Tigre, whose name is Spanish for tiger, lived up to his name and fought back with a vengeance. He bit the gator several times and managed to get free of the attacker's deadly grip. Then Alarcon waded into the water, grabbed the leash, and pulled Tigre to safety while the gator swam away.

Tigre was taken to the Christina Animal Hospital and treated for scrapes on his body and puncture wounds to his hind legs. It took several days for him to recover. Although he sported battle scars from the attack, Tigre no doubt left his own marks on the gator. He bit the reptile so hard that he broke one tooth and loosened two others.

Three years earlier in Florida, a Labrador-Doberman mix named Princess was nearly gator bait, but she, too, escaped death to bark another day.

During a family outing, owners Kirk and Julie Balliette let Princess take a dip in Lake Heron in the town of Bartow. Moments after Princess had paddled about 15 feet from shore, Julie noticed the silhouette of an alligator. "I just saw the ripple come up around her, and the gator just snatched her," she told the local newspaper, the *Lakeland Ledger*.

The alligator, estimated to be eight feet long, had the big dog's shoulder in its mouth and was trying to drag Princess under the surface. Julie said the terrified dog looked at her as if begging for help.

"I said, 'Fight, Princess, fight! Swim hard!'"

For 20 seconds, Princess did just that, thrashing and trying to free herself from the gator's deadly jaws. "She was howling and I was screaming," Julie recalled. She said she shouted, clapped her hands, splashed the water, and made noise, hoping to scare the alligator. "Somehow she got out."

Balliette and her oldest daughter, Sunny, 19, rushed their seven-year-old dog to the vet, where she needed only one staple to close a wound.

Dr. David Lee, Princess's veterinarian at the Edgewood Animal Clinic in Lakeland, told the newspaper that alligators are "a lot stronger and faster, and usually dogs don't win" in a matchup between pooch and gator.

To honor Princess's survival, Kirk Balliette wrapped the dog in orange and blue bandages, the colors of the University of Florida Gators. "She's our gator girl," he said. "She's earned her stripes."

Lost and Found

SNOW CAT

A nine-month-old kitten named Piper survived for a month trapped inside a snow-covered culvert. And he owes his life to a cat's archenemy — a dog.

Piper went missing from his home in snowbound Sault Ste. Marie, Ontario, Canada, in December 2009 after his owner, Verna Decaire, let him out at night. When he failed to show up the next morning, she started walking the neighborhood calling his name. Decaire and her family continued to search for the kitten over the next few weeks, but there was no sign of him.

"My son R.J. was very upset," Decaire told the local newspaper, the *Sault Star*. "Well, we all were. I kept telling R.J. one of the neighbors had probably picked him up, and he is warm and safe, and we are going to keep praying for him."

The truth was that Decaire feared Piper had frozen to death or been killed by a wild animal. But she never gave up hope. "I kept praying he would come home, or we would hear someone took in a cat and it might be him," she said.

Thirty days later, Decaire and her daughter Brittany were getting ready to go shopping when they saw neighbor Mary Hicks walking her dog, Aili, a seven-month-old German shepherd. As they chatted in the front yard, Aili feverishly began digging a hole in the snow that had piled up in the culvert at the end of the Decaires' driveway.

"She kept digging and digging," Hicks told the newspaper. "I was trying to get her away, but she kept dragging me back. She must have dug down about three feet. The only thing you could see was her behind and her tail."

After Aili dug a large hole in the snow, Hicks eventually pulled her dog away and continued their walk. Decaire went into the garage to start the car while Brittany waited outside.

Moments later, Brittany heard a screech and assumed it was a bird. When the sound grew louder, she realized it was coming from beneath the ground. "Just then a cat crawled out of the hole the dog had dug," Decaire recalled.

It was none other than Piper, who had lost weight since he had disappeared.

"I was in the garage, but Brittany was screaming, 'Mom! Mom!' I ran to her, and as she turned toward me, I could see the cat and I started screaming at the top of my lungs," said Decaire.

They bundled up the kitten and rushed him into the house to warm him up. The first thing he did was run to the bathroom to drink out of the toilet, a longtime habit of his.

When R.J. returned home from school that afternoon, he was overjoyed by his kitten's return. "He yelled, 'Piper, I knew you would come home,'" said Decaire. Piper spent his first night at home sleeping with R.J.

Even though Piper lost weight during the month-long ordeal, he made a full recovery.

"I think it is a miracle," Decaire said. "I cannot even comprehend being in a little closed space for all that time and having the will to keep on living."

WATERLOGGED SEADOG

Santos the dog slipped off a sailboat at sea and wasn't discovered missing until the next morning. His grief-stricken owners assumed he had drowned.

Were they in for a surprise!

The small, frisky, black pooch was the pet of Peter

and Dorothy Muilenburg and their son—a family who loved sailing to different ports of call along the Caribbean and South American coasts aboard their boat, *Breath*.

Santos was a Schipperkes, a type of dog whose ancestors were bred to serve aboard barges in Belgium. The dogs would swim ashore in the canals to nip at the heels of slow tow horses and also would bark if anyone fell overboard.

When the Muilenburgs first got Santos, they worried that he wasn't suited for life aboard a boat. That's because before he was three months old, Santos had almost drowned twice. The first time, he was running on the deck when he dashed right off the boat. His owners heard scratching on the hull and found the dog treading water, so they fished him out. A month later, while the boat was anchored offshore, Santos accidentally plunged into the water again, only to have the ebb tide carry him out to sea. A startled skin diver found him paddling in the ocean and returned him to his owners.

Once he outgrew puppyhood, Santos managed to stay topside and avoid further dunkings—until that fateful night in 1991 when he slipped and fell overboard five miles off the Venezuelan coast.

The Muilenburgs didn't discover he was missing until the next morning after they had anchored at Puerto Azul. They went ashore to report their heartbreaking loss to the port captain, who was busy supervising a sport-fishing tournament. He offered no encouragement, but promised to alert the fishermen to keep an eye out for Santos. The couple then went to a nearby bar and reminisced about their wonderful pet and how much they would miss him.

Wrote Peter Muilenburg in *Sail* magazine, "'Oh, well,' I consoled Dorothy. 'With that dog's temperament, we were lucky to have him as long as we did.' Dorothy's eyes brimmed. 'He was such a dear little dog. To think of him out there all alone!' A tear started down her cheek.

"Then we heard a shout from the port captain. 'You won't believe it,' he said. 'I just called the fishing boats on the radio to tally their standings for the scoreboard. And the last boat said they caught nothing—except a little black dog!'"

Someone on board the boat had spotted Santos bobbing in the ocean and scooped up the pooch with a hand net.

"Back on board *Breath*, Santos received a joyous welcome and got his own helping of the family dinner," said Muilenburg. "But his eyes were glazed as if they'd seen the whole of his life pass before them. Right after supper, he crashed."

Muilenburg wondered whether Santos's brush with death would make a more sensible animal of him. The next day, the skipper got his answer. Seeing kids playing on the beach with a German shepherd, Santos leaped into the sea and paddled toward the action.

SHIPPED OUT

A house cat named Spice spent nearly three weeks trapped inside a sealed shipping container with no food or water . . . and emerged in decent shape.

Her owner, Pamela Escamilla, of Waikoloa Village, Hawaii, was packing a large container of household goods in 2007 for a move to Southern California. After the container was locked and picked up for shipment, Escamilla couldn't find her three-year-old calico anywhere. She and her husband looked for several days, but had to call off their search because they needed to make their flight to the mainland. Before leaving, they asked neighbors to call them at their new residence in California if Spice showed up.

But Spice couldn't return to her home, because she had sneaked unnoticed into the Escamillas' shipping container while it was being packed. The container was put aboard a ship that sailed across the ocean to California. Entombed in the pitch-black, locked container, Spice had nothing but her will to survive to keep her alive.

When the container was brought to her new home, Escamilla opened it. She and family members noticed tufts of cat hair on the floor. Up until then, "it never even crossed my mind that she'd be in that container." But now Escamilla wondered, *Could it be that Spice is in there?* "We didn't know what we would find," she told the *Honolulu Star-Bulletin*.

"We really thought that cat was going to be dead," said Edward Gardner, Escamilla's father.

They started removing items until Escamilla was able to climb inside to search. Suddenly, she saw Spice poke her head out from behind some bicycles. "I started to scream," she recalled. Escamilla gently picked up the scared cat and took her to a veterinarian, who said Spice had some kidney and bowel problems. But considering what she had been through, the cat was in good condition.

Escamilla said the veterinarian told her that calicos have a strong survival instinct. "It's always a good day when the cat's alive," she said.

* * *

A year earlier, a stowaway white cat survived 17 days in a sealed shipping container.

The stray had wandered undetected into a container that was being loaded with plastic goods in Afula, Israel. After the container was closed, the cat took an unexpected 2,300-mile ocean voyage to England without any food or water. Two and a half weeks after the container had been sent on its way, it was finally opened in Whitworth, Lancashire, England.

"The staff unloading it got a real surprise when this fluffy white cat shot out," Colin Barton, the local authority's animal-health officer, told the *Manchester Evening News*.

Even though the cat was starving and dehydrated, he managed to avoid getting caught for another five hours. "I think he was scared to death," said James Ratcliff, of the Royal SPCA. "He'd traveled all that way . . . and ran for his life."

Royal SPCA officers nabbed the cat by a pool of water on the warehouse roof, tempting him with a plate of tuna fish. He was taken to an animal clinic, where he recovered from his ordeal.

Workers decided to name the skinny white cat Ziggy after Ziggy Stardust, the character created by rock star David Bowie in the 1970s, because the cat had one green eye and one blue eye, just like Bowie.

A HOLE LOT OF TROUBLE

Judy the Jack Russell terrier puppy disappeared down a rabbit hole and didn't come out until she was rescued—five weeks later!

In 1990, Evan Davies, 11, of San Antonio, Texas, was walking Judy when she broke loose and chased a rabbit into its warren. Evan waited for his dog to return, but she didn't. The family assumed she somehow had died in the rabbit hole or had found another way out and was lost.

"Evan went out every day to the rabbit hole, looking for Judy," his mother, Jean, told reporters. "Even though we'd all given up hope of ever seeing Judy again, Evan just wouldn't believe she was dead."

Finally, 36 days later, a neighbor walking by the rabbit hole heard a faint whimper coming from under the ground. He got a shovel and began digging. Suddenly, out popped a dirty, skinny, brown and white puppy.

"It was Judy," recalled Evan. "I knew she was there somewhere, just waiting to be found. She was hungry and thirsty, but she was fine. She won't be going near any more holes."

BLOWIN' IN THE WIND

Tinker Bell, a five-pound Chihuahua, lived up to her name when she flew off like a fairy. Unlike the *Peter Pan* fable, though, this Tinker Bell was whisked away by a bad tornadolike storm.

Dorothy Utley and her husband, Lavern, of Rochester, Michigan, were setting up an outdoor display at a flea market in Waterford Township near Detroit in 2009. Their eight-month-old long-haired black and brown dog was tethered to the back of a trailer. Within minutes, a terrible storm roared through the area. During the height of the tempest, a 70-mile-per-hour gust of wind picked up Tinker Bell and sent her airborne until she was out of sight.

"She just went," Dorothy told the *Detroit News*. "The wind came up and within seconds she was gone."

Joe Goldberg, manager of the Dixieland Flea Market where the Utleys were regular vendors, said he saw Tinker Bell blow away when he went outside to survey the damage caused by the hurricane-force gusts. "I saw a flash," he told ABCNews.com. "It lifted off. Gone. This dog was picked up at least sixty feet in the air. Dorothy said, 'My dog blew away,' and forty people ran over."

Many of the vendors closed for the day to help the Utleys search for their dog, while others worked to clean up the wind damage to the flea market. Goldberg said that people lost what amounted to a day's pay to look for little Tinker Bell.

"We found her leash on the highway, which is a six-lane highway, and we went all around looking, but she just wasn't there," said Lavern Utley. The couple searched the area for two days, but other than the leash, there were no signs of Tinker Bell.

Two days later, a local pet psychic called them and suggested they look in woods about a mile from the flea market for their dog. Figuring they had nothing to lose but time, the Utleys went to the location. "I went up to a hill in the woods and was probably there for around a half hour, calling her name," Utley recalled. "She just came running to me. She wasn't hurt or anything. She was fine, just had some mud on her."

Tinker Bell was overjoyed to see her owners again. "That dog was so happy, she just went wild," Dorothy said. "We were shocked when we found her. You don't know how happy we were. We love her so much."

* * *

Like Toto in the classic movie *The Wizard of Oz*, Sadie the Yorkshire terrier was sucked into the sky by a tornado.

In 1993, Sadie was playing alone in the yard while her owners, James and Sandra Davis, of Saginaw, Texas, were at work. Suddenly, a twister roared through the neighborhood and slammed into the Davises' house.

Minutes later, the couple rushed home and discovered that their house suffered heavy damage, later estimated at $60,000. But their first concern was for Sadie, a Christmas present given five years earlier to their daughter, Lindsay, when she was three.

"When we first came home and saw all the pieces of fence and roof and decking all over the place, we started pulling them up looking for Sadie," recalled James.

Then the Davises searched around the neighborhood, but still couldn't find her.

"One of our neighbors came up to me and asked what was I looking for," said Sandra. "I told her Sadie, and she asked, 'Was it brown and white?' I said, 'Yes.' And she said that she had seen the tornado pick up a brown and white furry ball. When it was twenty feet in the air, she realized it was a little dog. My heart just sank."

Learning that Sadie had been carried off by the twister, the Davises figured she probably had been killed. But they still held out a little hope that she had survived the tornado, so they combed the countryside. Unfortunately, they weren't successful.

However, the next day, their despair turned to joy. They received a call from a man who had found their four-pound terrier shortly after the storm, wandering by the side of a road two miles from her home. Luckily, the dog had been wearing a name tag with the Davises' phone number on it.

Except for a few ant bites, Sadie appeared to be fine.

"We were so thrilled when we got her back," said James at the time. "She's like a member of our family. Surviving that tornado was nothing short of a miracle."

CURIOSITY NEARLY KILLED THE CAT

Molly the black cat was a little too curious for her own good. While snooping around the basement of a deli where she lived, she wiggled her way into a crawl space behind a brick wall and became stuck for two weeks without food or water.

The 11-month-old cat had been adopted by Peter Myers, owner of a New York deli called Myers of

Keswick. Molly, who was allowed to roam in the shop, was a favorite of customers and a good mouser. One evening in 2006 as he closed up shop for the day, Myers left food for Molly and whistled for her. She didn't show up, so he assumed she was snoozing somewhere in the back.

Not seeing her the next day, he wondered if Molly had slipped out the door. He asked neighbors if they had spotted her, but no one had. While whistling for her in front of his shop, Myers heard a faint meow coming from behind a wall between his building and the one next door.

He called the fire department and was told there was nothing they could do. Then he got in touch with Animal Care & Control, a private organization with a city contract to handle lost, injured, and unwanted animals. They tried to coax Molly out with open cans of food. As word spread, volunteers and neighbors offered help. They even brought kittens, hoping the mewing would trigger her motherly instincts and motivate her to leave.

Any one of those ideas might have worked had Molly been able to move. Not until the rescuers used a special miniature camera at the end of a plumber's snake did they learn that the cat was stuck between beams and pipes sandwiched between two old buildings. Still unsure exactly where she was, they began drilling holes and hammering out bricks in the ceiling and walls.

As the days passed, Molly's plight captured the imagination of New York. Newspaper reporters, TV crews, and photographers gathered daily to chronicle the efforts of rescue workers who worried that time would run out before they could reach her. They were heartened, though, that her distressed meows were still easily heard.

Molly was finally retrieved by Kevin Clifford, a tunnel worker at a project nearby, who had devoted dozens of hours of his own time to rescue her. "I gave what was needed and lent a hand," he told reporters.

The cat didn't come out easily at first, said Mike Pastore, field director for Animal Care & Control. "She was twisting and turning, and paws were flying everywhere," he said. "It took a little struggle."

She had managed to get lodged up high by the ceiling of the shop about 15 feet from the front of the building.

After 14 days trapped in the innards of the Greenwich Village building, Molly finally emerged, appearing somewhat frazzled, but unhurt despite her ordeal. She remained fairly calm as the media and paparazzi crowded around her. "I think you'll agree she's in great shape," a relieved Myers told the press. "I'm amazed at how well she looks. She always was a fit cat, otherwise she wouldn't have survived fourteen days in that hole."

For her first meal of freedom, he gave her roasted pork, sardines in oil, and water.

Molly's rescue made big news in New York. It was even announced at a New York Mets home game. She appeared on *Regis and Kelly* and *Good Day New York*, and her story made all the local TV stations as well as CNN.

Unfortunately, the shop had been left in a shambles because of all the drilling and holes. But cat lovers donated money to help pay for the repairs.

Molly didn't lose her job as a mouser and remained at the deli, where she became an instant celebrity. Myers admitted, however, "I look at the cat every night and think, 'Does she know the stress she caused me?'"

PIPE DOWN

A pet cat was stuck in a sealed storm drainpipe for 16 days before she was freed.

A curious kitty named Chloe was snooping around a construction site near her home in Blenheim, New

Zealand, in 2002. On that day workers were capping off the exposed ends of an underground seven-inch-wide storm-water pipe to prevent animals and debris from slipping into it during a heavy rain.

It was also on that day that Chloe disappeared. When she failed to return home, her owners, Lesley and Allan Butland, searched the neighborhood, put up posters, and called animal shelters and agencies to no avail.

They had no way of knowing that Chloe had been buried alive in a pipe three feet below the ground.

For 16 days, the 13-year-old feline paced up and down the dark and slender tube and mewed her heart out for help. She was able to stay alive by lapping up droplets of water seeping through a gap in the cap of the pipe. Day after day, Chloe continued to meow . . . until finally someone heard her.

According to the *Marlborough Express*, when construction worker Michael Birtwistle arrived at the work site, he heard the cat's cries. Birtwistle and two workers uncapped the pipe and peered inside. They discovered a bedraggled and scrawny Chloe, who was so sick and weak that she couldn't move. The pads of her paws had become completely worn down from constant pacing. Half of her fur was gone, she had lost over half of her weight, and she appeared temporarily blind.

The rescuers had to use a piece of hooked wire to catch her collar and pull her limp body out of the pipe. The cat was taken to a nearby veterinary clinic, where nurses were shocked to discover that her temperature was so low that it wouldn't even register on a thermometer. She was put on a heated intravenous drip and given doses of vitamins and minerals.

Because her owners had been so diligent in trying to find Chloe, the clinic was able to contact them right away. "She was in a pretty sorry state," Lesley Butland told the newspaper. "She was a big cat, and she lost half of her body weight. When they washed her, she looked like a rat." But she pulled through. "She is a courageous wee cat."

Hard Times

A WHALE OF A TIME

A whale that was hopelessly entangled in a web of crab-pot lines survived by remaining calm while divers worked to free her. She was so grateful when they succeeded that she "thanked" each one of them.

The 50-foot female humpback, estimated to weigh 50 tons, was on her usual migratory route between the Northern California coast and Baja California in 2005 when she unintentionally swam into 20 nylon ropes that linked crab pots. Each rope was 240 feet long with weights every 60 feet. Rope was wrapped at least four times around her tail, back, and left front flipper. Another line was tugging in her mouth. The crab-pot lines were cinched so tight that they were digging into the animal's blubber, leaving visible cuts. Adding to her woes, she was seriously hampered by at least 12 crab traps, each weighing 90 pounds, that hung off her. Their weight was pulling her downward, forcing her to struggle mightily to keep her blowhole out of the water.

She was spotted by a crab fisherman in the open water east of the Farallon Islands, about 18 miles off the coast of San Francisco.

Hours later, volunteer divers for the Marine Mammal Center of Marin County reached the distressed endangered whale and realized the only way to save her was to dive into the water and cut the ropes. Such an undertaking carried huge risks for the divers because a flip of a humpback's massive tail can kill a person.

"I was the first diver in the water, and my heart sank when I saw all the lines wrapped around it," diver James Moskito told the *San Francisco Chronicle*. "I really didn't think we were going to be able to save it."

Moskito and three other divers spent about an hour cutting the ropes with a special curved knife. The whale floated passively in the water the whole time, he said, giving off a strange kind of vibration.

Humpback whales are known for their complex vocalizations that sound like singing and for their acrobatic breaching in which they lift almost their entire bodies out of the water and splash down.

"When I was cutting the line that was going through its mouth, its eye was there winking at me, watching me," Moskito said. "It seemed kind of affectionate, like a dog that's happy to see you. I never felt threatened. It was an amazing, unbelievable experience."

Once she was freed, the humpback gently nudged her rescuers one at a time and flapped around in what marine experts said was a rare and remarkable encounter. "It felt to me like it was thanking us, knowing that it was free and that we had helped it," Moskito said. "It stopped about a foot away from me, pushed me around a little bit, and had some fun."

Mick Menigoz, who was part of the effort that saved the humpback, told the newspaper, "The whale was doing little dives, and the guys were rubbing shoulders with it. I don't know for sure what it was thinking, but it's something that I will always remember. It was just too cool."

"The daring rescue was the first successful attempt on the West Coast to free an entangled humpback," said Shelbi Stoudt, stranding manager for the Marine Mammal Center.

DEFROSTED

Annie the cat was found in a snowbank frozen stiff and lifeless. She was then literally thawed out . . . and came back to life.

The 13-year-old tuxedo cat had disappeared a week

after her owners moved to their new home in Norfolk, Massachusetts, in December 2009. The family put up "Missing Cat" fliers and contacted animal control. But after several weeks of searching, the owners lost hope they would ever see their gray and white pet again, especially when temperatures plunged below zero.

Five weeks after she vanished, someone found an extremely thin, frozen cat in a snowbank near a busy intersection. The poor animal appeared dead, so Norfolk Animal Control Officer Hilary Cohen was called to the scene.

"Basically, when I picked her up, she had no signs of life," Cohen told the local newspaper, *The Sun Chronicle*. "She was stiff, she was unconscious, cold to the touch and not responding to anything."

Even though the cat was lifeless, Cohen decided to take her to the Acorn Animal Hospital to be sure. "I kept her in the blanket and put her on my lap in the cruiser," she told Boston's WBZ-TV. "Once in the car, I turned the heaters on and saw a whisker twitch. That was really the only sign of life I saw from her."

When the cat was brought in, she weighed only three pounds and had a temperature of just 86 degrees, which was far below the normal 101 degrees. She was in a deep coma but at least she was still alive. The question was, would she stay alive? The veterinary staff tried heat therapy, IV fluids, blood sugar monitoring, and steroids to revive the cat. Within a few hours, the cat emerged from her coma.

"The staff worked miracles on this little cat," Cohen said.

Days after her rescue, the cat seemed back to her old self. She was walking, eating, and drinking. Because she was so affectionate, Cohen knew the cat was someone's pet.

After the *Sun Chronicle* published an article about the thawed-out cat, her owner read the story and contacted Cohen. The owner was able to prove that the miracle cat was indeed Annie, or at least a shadow of her former self, because she had lost so much weight.

Said the owner, who asked not to be named, "She had a strong heart and a strong will to live that was just incredible."

RIDING THE RAILS

A stowaway kitten clung to the underside of a speeding train for a terrifying 900 miles.

The four-week-old black kitty was seen leaping into the undercarriage of a Chiltern Railways diesel train in England in 2009. An engineer looked for him but couldn't find him and assumed the cat had dashed off. But the kitten *hadn't* fled. He then traveled between London Marylebone and the West Midlands at least five times over a 24-hour period. And even though the train zoomed through the countryside at speeds of more than 100 miles an hour, amazingly the kitten never fell off.

During the train's run back and forth, the engineers heard what sounded like a meow coming from underneath the door of the engineer's cab. When the train stopped in Wembley, they found the cat perched in a gear box area close to the wheels.

"It managed to stay there for nine hundred miles and not fall off—it is absolutely amazing," Chiltern Railways spokeswoman Emma Gascoigne told London's *Daily Mail.*

After being enticed out with a slice of salami, the kitten was taken to a vet, who gave him a clean bill of health. The cat was then returned to the railroad company, where workers put him in a box.

"When I got to work in the morning, I was asked whether I wanted a cat," employee Jodi Fox told the newspaper. "I thought it was a joke, but then I looked inside the box and I fell in love with him straightaway. He just looked so cute.

"I was really shocked when I heard what had

happened. He would have been able to see the tracks where he was, and he must have been petrified."

It was a scary and dangerous way to find a new home, but at least he got one. Fox adopted the kitten and named him, fittingly, Diesel.

WHEN SOMETHING BAD
TURNED OUT GOOD

A stray dog was run over by a freight train, not once but twice — and believe it or not, that was probably a good thing.

Fred Krause, an engineer for a Utah Railway Company, was operating a train one night in 2010 near Salt Lake City when he noticed a small cream-colored dog lying in the tracks. It was too late to stop the train. Seconds before the train ran over it, the pooch hunched down between the rails.

Krause wasn't sure whether the dog was struck or not, but hoped the mutt was small enough to avoid being hit.

On the return of his 16-mile run later that night, Krause spotted the dog at the same spot. This time, the pooch was running on the tracks in front of the train. The engineer blew his whistle and slowed the train from 20 miles per hour to 15 miles per hour, but there was no way the dog could outrun it. Krause heard the dog get hit by the snowplow that was on the front of the engine.

After arriving at his destination, Krause returned by vehicle to the spot where he had hit the dog. "My heart went out to the little guy, and I had to go back and look," he told the Ogden *Standard-Examiner*. The engineer feared the dog was dead or had its legs cut off, and he would have to put it down. "The last thing I expected was to find him alive."

The dog, an older male Shih Tzu, was very much alive, although dazed and still lying between the rails. "He looked like he had his bell rung. pretty good," Krause said. "He was obviously in shock."

Krause picked him up and took him to a veterinarian, who said the dog suffered a concussion. The pooch also had health issues that had nothing to do with the accident, including overexposure to the winter elements, infections in his feet and eyes, and a heart murmur. Based on his matted hair, the eight-pound Shih Tzu had not been cared for in some time.

Krause, who already owned a Shih Tzu, named Milo, brought the new dog home in Clinton, Utah, to nurse him back to health. The engineer and his wife, Lori, named the dog the Little Guy.

Ironically, if the dog hadn't been struck by the train, he probably wouldn't have survived the rest of the winter.

"It was a good thing Fred had clocked him in the head with the train," said Lori. A heavy snowstorm blanketed the area days after he was found. Krause said that between the harsh weather and the plentiful foxes, the Little Guy wouldn't have stood much of a chance of surviving.

With loving care from the Krauses, the Shih Tzu gained weight and recovered from his ailments, no doubt thankful that he got hit by a train.

TIGHT SQUEEZE

A plucky cat was trapped in a three-inch-wide space between two buildings for nearly two years!

Incredibly, he survived.

The tabby belonged to the John Poppelaurer family, who lived on the top floor of a four-story apartment building in New York City. In 1902, when he was still a kitten who had yet to be named, he fell off the roof and down into a gap that separated the building with the one next door. The kitten survived the plunge, but couldn't get out of the confining space, which had brick walls on both sides. Every time he began climbing the bricks, he slipped and fell.

Residents tried to rescue the kitten by rigging poles together and putting them down to the bottom of the gap in the hope that he would crawl up onto them. Unfortunately, their efforts failed. Pieces of meat were fastened to string, which was lowered in an attempt to catch the kitten like a fish. But that didn't work, either.

The poor kitty wasn't happy. He yowled day and night. After a week, the neighbors were divided into two camps—those who wanted to shoot or poison the kitten to put him out of his misery, and those who believed that as long as the feline was alive, there was hope for his rescue. The cat lovers prevailed, and named the kitten Holey, after the hole he had put himself in. Every day they dropped food to him, and every night a woman lowered a can of water for him.

Meanwhile, Holey continued to grow, but because of the confining three-inch-wide space, his body remained more or less squished.

News of the cat's predicament finally reached the SPCA. "The agent who came to investigate was for killing the cat," reported the *New York Times*. "The [cat lovers] almost mobbed him for his cruel point of view. He suggested shooting it, but the cat's friends argued that he might thus jeopardize the safety of the occupants of the two houses." Despite their protests, the agent dropped poisoned liver down to Holey, but the cat was smart enough not to eat it. "The agent finally gave up," said the *Times*.

In 1904, nearly two years after Holey had tumbled into the gap, a cowboy who had been visiting New York heard about the cat and came to the rescue. An expert at handling the lariat, the cowboy went out onto the roof and lowered his rope. After a few tries, he lassoed Holey by the neck and then dragged the snarling, spitting, choking feline up to the top.

So what did the cat do after 23 months of imprisonment? The moment Holey was freed from the rope and revived from choking, he made a mad dash to get back into the gap. Apparently, the cat was afraid of his suddenly spacious environment and of the humans who had kept him alive.

But Holey was caught before he had a chance to dive between the buildings. The cat—whose misshapen body looked like it had been squeezed in a vice (which, in a way, it had been)—was carried into the Poppelaurers' apartment, where he nervously paced back and forth. It took several days before he calmed down, and eventually he settled into a quiet life as a house cat—a very compressed house cat.

GO WITH THE FLOE

Somehow a cute mongrel ended up a lonely castaway for at least four days on an ice floe that had drifted miles out into the Baltic Sea.

The dog's frozen odyssey happened in 2010 during one of Poland's bitter winter cold snaps, with temperatures dipping to minus 4 degrees. The brown and black mutt was first spotted on an ice floe floating down the Vistula River 60 miles inland in the town of Grudziadz. Firefighters tried to save him, but couldn't reach him because the ice sheets were shifting.

Days later, the thick-furred male dog was found adrift 15 miles out in the Baltic Sea by the crew of the *Baltica*, a Polish ship carrying ocean scientists. Surprised to see a dog shivering on an ice floe so far from land, the crew immediately tried to save him.

Researcher Natalia Drgas told reporters that the rescue was difficult. "It was a tough struggle. The dog kept slipping into the water and crawling back on top of the ice. At one point he vanished underwater, under the ship, and we thought it was the end. But he emerged again and crawled on an ice sheet."

Fearing he could drown, the crew lowered a pontoon into the water. The ship's mechanic, Adam Buczynski, rowed it to the ice floe and managed to grab the frightened dog by the scruff of the neck and pull him to safety.

Jerzy Wosachlo, the captain of the *Baltica*, told reporters the dog slept on a blanket in the ship's laboratory and later shared a sausage breakfast with the crew. He said the dog stuck close to Buczynski at first, but eventually started making friends with the rest of the crew, who gave the pooch the name Baltic.

"We have enrolled him as a crew member," Wosachlo said.

When the ship arrived in the port of Gdynia, the 44-pound dog was taken to a veterinarian, who found Baltic in surprisingly good condition and estimated the mutt was about six years old. The vet said a dog with thick fur and a layer of fat can survive cold conditions for as long as eight days if it has water to drink.

While the ship was still in port, Baltic was occasionally taken on land for walks. The Sea Fishing Institute, which owned the ship, sent a bowl and a squeaking toy while the scientists on board brought dog food.

After news broke of the dog's rescue, Wosachlo received numerous calls from people as far away as Australia and Canada offering money to feed the dog or wanting to adopt him. Two people showed up at the dock, claiming Baltic was theirs. But the pooch kept his distance from them and showed no signs that he recognized them.

A Facebook page was set up to provide people throughout the world updates and photos of Baltic. Two months after the rescue, Ewa Baradziej-Krzyzankowska, the dog's spokeswoman who works for the Sea Fisheries Institute, wrote in Facebook, "Baltic is doing very, very well, is loved, and is being spoiled rotten by the entire crew and Mr. Adam Buczynski, who is taking care of him. He loves to walk in the woods and to be on the boat."

Polish President Lech Kaczynski, who was a dog owner, sent the crew a letter praising its action in saving Baltic's life. "Such gestures make our world a better one," Kaczynski wrote.

A FLOORED FELINE

A black cat had the bad luck of being trapped for two months under a concrete floor of a building under construction.

The cat might never have survived had it not been for a surprise visit by health and safety inspectors. During an examination of the site in Newquay, Cornwall, England, in 2004, inspectors Steve Jones and Jonathan Harris heard faint meowing coming from under a block-and-beam concrete floor that had been laid eight weeks earlier. Site manager Mark Tanner then instructed workers to break open a hole in the floor. When they did, a skinny black cat scampered out.

"It was certainly the worse for wear, but not actually harmed," Charles Gilby, another inspector, told the BBC.

After being given some water, which he eagerly lapped up, the feline was turned over to the Royal SPCA. At the shelter, an examination revealed he was underweight and dehydrated. He apparently survived on droplets of moisture.

Animal-collection officer Felicity Cross believed the cat, which was about 10 years old, had been trying to escape. "His claws are really scuffed and broken, which suggests he's been scrabbling around trying to find a way out," she told the BBC.

Shelter workers gave the cat the name Houdini.

DOWN THE DRAIN

A puppy was flushed down the toilet by a well-meaning little boy . . . and survived.

In Northolt, Middlesex, England, in 2009, Alison

Blair presented her children with a new cocker spaniel puppy. A week later, after taking their pet for a family walk, four-year-old Daniel decided that the pup needed a bath because his paws were dirty. Daniel and his brother took the dog—who was still so new he had yet to have a name—into the bathroom.

"I realized the dog was missing and asked the boys where he was," their mother told London's *Daily Mirror*. "Daniel told me the dog had got muddy so they put him in the toilet and pulled the chain to give him a wash. I ran into the bathroom but the dog was nowhere to be seen. I assumed he was dead. I went into the garden, managed to lift up the drain cover, and was amazed to hear him crying."

Blair called the fire brigade and Royal SPCA, but after three hours of trying, neither could get the poor pup out. She then called Dyno-Rod, a plumbing company.

"We took a call from a distressed lady from North London saying, 'Please help me. I don't know what to do. The fire brigade is here, and they can't do it,'" Dyno-Rod engineer Will Craig told London's *Telegraph*.

"All we were concerned about was getting the puppy out alive," Craig said. Plumbers used a special tiny camera that was threaded into the drain pipe to locate the little pooch. The dog was lying upside down in the pipe 20 yards away under a neighbor's house. Neighbors on the block were asked not to flush their toilets while the rescue was under way, to prevent the puppy from being carried away by wastewater into the main sewer.

When he located the puppy he nudged him along with the camera through the drainage system. "It took a while, but eventually I got him to the next manhole, where a fireman was waiting to pull him out. Luckily the puppy was unhurt, and he is apparently getting on well," said Craig.

Commenting on the success of the rescue effort, Craig added, "You know, it just makes you feel good."

As for little Daniel, he told the *Daily Mirror*, "I had to give him a wash. I'm so, so sorry. I won't do it again."

Added his mother, "I never thought a dog could survive being flushed down the loo [toilet]. He's a real little fighter."

In honor of the plumbing company that saved the puppy's life, the family named the dog Dyno.

COMPACT PUPPY

A female puppy ended up in a garbage truck's compactor that was crushing tons of cardboard. Miraculously, the Labrador–pit bull mix survived with barely a scratch.

The truck made five stops at cardboard trash bins in and around Evansville, Indiana, in 2008. At one of those stops, the dog had either climbed into a bin or been tossed into one by a cruel person. Unfortunately for the puppy, the driver didn't know she was buried in the cardboard. After emptying the contents of each bin into the truck, the driver turned on the truck's compactor—a ramming device that crushed the cardboard with 35,000 pounds of pressure.

The truck then drove to the Smurfit-Stone recycling company in Evansville. When equipment operator Dan Vallier started clearing out the three-ton load of crushed cardboard from the truck, he couldn't believe what he saw. "In between some cardboard, I saw her head poking out," he told reporters.

He bolted to her aid and pulled her out. To everyone's surprise, all she had was a bruised foot, said plant manager Kevin Hines. "She was very lucky," he added. "It pretty much meant it should have been the end of her, but it wasn't."

Hines said that because the puppy was found in the middle of the crushed cardboard, she probably endured at least two or three cycles of the truck's compactor. It was probably because she was totally surrounded by cardboard that she survived the compactor's powerful ramming.

"We find all kinds of things in the trash, like toilets and things," said Vallier. "But we sure don't expect to see a puppy, especially one that lived."

Because the workers had already adopted a stray cat, they decided against keeping the puppy as a mascot. Instead, they fed her, bathed her, and gave her flea powder. Then they found a family to adopt her.

"We thought if she made it through this, she deserved a good home," said Hines.

Big Falls

JUMPING-OFF PLACE

For a reason that only he would know—and he wasn't talking—a one-year-old standard poodle named Brodie leaped over a guard rail into the Elora Gorge in Ontario, Canada. He plunged more than 100 feet, bouncing off a limestone cliff on the way down, before splashing into the swift Grand River below and getting swept away.

And yet he lived with hardly any injuries.

"We were in shock," Malcolm Molloy told reporters later. He; his wife, Diane; and their two children had been walking Brodie along a trail by the gorge in 2002. "The dog just took off and leaped right over the wall," Molloy recalled. "By the time I got to the ledge, I saw him hit the edge of the cliff about ten feet off the river. He flipped over and landed in the water."

Brodie had survived the fall, but was now thrashing about in the icy rapids below. While Molloy frantically was making his way down to the water, he yelled to two kayakers, a man and a woman in their late 20s, asking for their help.

Acting quickly, the male kayaker caught up with the battered, waterlogged dog. "[The kayaker] had managed to grab hold of him, but the river was running full-fledged," Molloy said. "When I talked to him later, he said the dog had slipped away at first. He said Brodie went under two or three times, and he reckoned it would have been his last time going down, but he grabbed him again."

Eventually, the soaked pooch was pulled out of the water, bruised and shivering, but well enough to wag his tail. Amazingly, Brodie suffered only a cut on his face, a fat lip, and some bruises.

DEATH-DEFYING THREE-TIMER

Buddy the cocker spaniel cheated death three times in one awful day after he twice fell off a cliff and then nearly drowned a mile out at sea.

"I can't believe he went through all of that and lived to tell the tale," his owner Steve Kingsley told London's *Daily Mail*. "It's a miracle really."

The five-year-old chocolate brown dog was on a walk with Kingsley along the cliffs overlooking Studland Bay, Dorset, England, in 2009. Buddy spotted a rabbit and chased after it. All of a sudden, he disappeared through the bushes and tumbled off the

100-foot-tall seaside cliff and splashed into the water.

"For a second I thought he was a goner," said Kingsley. "But I looked down, and he was paddling in the sea."

Uninjured by the fall, Buddy swam back to the base of the cliff, which was lined with rocks and a beach. Relieved that his dog was still alive, Kingsley began the 20-minute hike to the bottom. "I rushed down the path to the beach, and when I got there, there was no sign of him," he told the newspaper. "I searched all along the beach and feared he had drowned."

But then a hiker told Kingsley that Buddy was seen trying to climb the cliff. When he was about 30 feet up, the dog lost his footing and plummeted back into the water. Having taken two unwelcome plunges into the chilly water, Buddy decided that he wanted nothing more to do with the cliff. So to the dismay of his owner, Buddy started dog-paddling out to sea. He was last seen swimming toward the Isle of Wight.

Desperate to save him, Kingsley called the coast guard, who sent out a message for any boats in the area to be on the lookout for a cocker spaniel in the water.

Sailor Steve Moran and his wife, Annette, heard the alert on board their 46-foot ketch, the *Cordelia*, which was anchored about a mile away in Studland

Bay. With binoculars, the Morans soon spotted Buddy, who was exhausted and weak, bobbing in the sea. They rode out to him in a motorized raft and dragged him aboard. "He was quite distressed when we reached him and was whimpering," Steve Moran told the *Daily Mail*. "We took him back to our boat and gave him some water and some food, which we had for our Jack Russell. I was really surprised he was still alive, considering he fell off a 100-foot cliff and was in the water for about two hours."

After the couple informed the coast guard of the rescue, a Jet Skier rode out to their yacht to fetch Buddy and brought him back to the beach to his thrilled owner. "I couldn't believe he was still in one piece," Kingsley said. "He was absolutely fine and was full of the joys of spring.

"I only took him out for a quiet walk, and yet he managed to trigger this huge scare involving almost everyone on the beach and at sea. He is so lucky."

Guinness the bird dog took an unexpected dive off a cliff on the British coast.

In 1991, Guinness was walking with his human family, the Dightons, of Edenbridge, England, near the edge of a huge seaside cliff. Suddenly, "Guinness went racing past me, chasing a bird," ten-year-old Barry Jr. recalled. "I couldn't stop him."

The spaniel went sailing off the cliff, which rose 225 feet from a rocky beach below.

When he discovered what had happened, Barry Sr. fearfully looked over the edge, expecting to see Guinness's broken body on the rocks below. Luckily, the pooch had landed smack into the English Channel and was still alive. He began paddling toward shore when two startled fishermen, who saw his fall, plucked him from the water and returned him to his much-relieved owners.

What saved Guinness from certain death was the tide. "He was lucky it was high tide," said Barry Sr. "He could never have survived those rocks."

Nevertheless, the 225-foot plunge into the cold water left Guinness with injuries. The dog was taken to the animal clinic, where he was treated for internal bleeding and a damaged lung. However, he made a full recovery.

Meanwhile, the Dightons vowed never to walk near a cliff again with Guinness.

Mac, an 18-month-old golden retriever, was so intent on catching a fleeing rabbit along the top of a cliff that he failed to stop and went flying straight over the edge.

The dog plunged 40 feet onto seaside rocks. He broke both his legs and punctured a lung, but amazingly he lived.

Mac was walking on a leash with his owner, Margaret Sills, 65, on a coastal path in the Isle of Wight in the United Kingdom in 2009 when he spotted the rabbit. The bunny was just too tempting for Mac to resist, so the dog broke free from Sills's grip and charged after the animal. Running for its life, the rabbit bounded left and right, zigzagging its way toward the ocean. It dashed into a bush and was smart enough to stop just a few feet short of the cliff's edge.

Unfortunately, Mac, who was running at full speed, wasn't quite that smart. He couldn't stop and went flying before tumbling down the rocky slope.

Sills was horrified to see her dog soar off the edge. Fearing he was dead, she could hardly force herself to look over the side. "I couldn't believe it when he went over, but I was even more shocked he survived," she told the *Sun*, a British newspaper. "I still find it hard not to cry when I talk about it. He is the most amazing dog. Even on the rocks at the bottom of the cliff, as soon as he saw me, his little tail started wagging."

His life was spared by his leather collar, which

snagged on the rocks on the way down and slowed his descent.

"It saved his life," Sills told the *Daily Telegraph*. "If he hadn't been wearing one, he would have just free-fallen all the way, and there's no way he could have survived."

Although he was still alive, he was seriously hurt.

It took coast guard rescuers three and a half hours to reach Mac before he was taken to the local animal clinic. Four days later, he was transferred to Broadway Veterinary Hospital in Peterborough, England, near Sills's home.

Hayley Stevenson was among a team of nurses, critical-care vets, and orthopedic surgeons who helped Mac recover. "When Mac arrived with us, he had two fractured front legs and air in his chest and a massive amount of bruising," she told the newspaper. "In two separate operations we repaired Mac's fractures by inserting two metal plates and splints to support his legs. He's an amazing dog. Even with all the pain that he was in and not being able to walk, he was full of life and wagging his tail."

Sills, who had suffered four strokes, which made walking difficult, said Mac's survival meant everything to her. "He's my only companion at home, and he's my best friend," she told reporters at the time. "He makes a lot of things possible for me. If I can't get out of my chair, he comes over and supports me. He even picks up my mobile phone when I can't reach it, and I haven't even trained him to do it. Now it's my turn to go around picking things up for him, but I don't mind at all. I'm just so happy he's still here."

Sills, the grandmother of seven, said the six-month recovery cost her more than $2,000. "But Mac is well worth it."

FALL OUT

Some cats live life on the edge—and nearly die that way, too, by falling off balconies and ledges from dizzying heights.

For example, a seven-year-old Manx named Voodoo fell 34 floors from a penthouse in Runaway Bay, Queensland, Australia, and hardly had a scratch on him.

Voodoo had a habit of walking on the railing of the balcony of his owners, Wayne and Sheree Washington. One evening in 2008, they noticed that Voodoo was missing. "We searched high and low several times, and he was nowhere to be found," Wayne told the local newspaper *Gold Coast Bulletin*. "At one A.M., we went to bed."

Added Sheree, "It was a very daunting night and I figured if I found him, he wouldn't be alive."

The next morning, she went downstairs, expecting to find her dear cat's body at the base of the high rise. Instead, she found Voodoo with nothing more than a few scratches. "I just saw him lying under the bushes," she said. "He was just crouched back in the corner."

Luckily, Voodoo landed on a bush, breaking his fall and saving his life. Several branches were snapped, clearly indicating where Voodoo had landed. Sheree took her cat to the animal clinic, where he was treated for a bloodshot eye, a scratched ear, a cut mouth, and a damaged paw.

Wayne called Voodoo's survival "unbelievable." He told the newspaper, "I was convinced he was dead and we were going to bring him back for a burial. Instead we're going to have a celebration." In a classic understatement, he added, Voodoo is "a very lucky cat."

Speaking of Lucky, that was the name of a cat who was only slightly injured after a 26-story plunge from a Manhattan high rise in 2009. His dramatic fall was captured on camera by a window washer.

Lucky, a three-year-old gray and black tabby, was following his owner, Keri Hostetler, who was cleaning her thirty-second-floor apartment in preparation for guests. She cracked open a window about six inches to air out a room. With the room's door ajar, she left to do some laundry.

When she returned, she couldn't find Lucky. Then she saw the door open to the room that had the open window. "I ran around the apartment screaming for him," she told the TV show *Good Morning America Weekend Edition*. "And then I saw the window, and I knew what had happened."

When she went to the window, she saw two window washers on scaffolding about 30 stories high on a building directly across the street. They were frantically waving at her, as if trying to tell her something.

Moments earlier, they had seen Lucky slip out of the open window. "The cat was on the ledge, and we saw it trying to turn a corner," recalled window washer John Hayes. "But there was no other ledge for him to step on. My partner told me to get my camera, so I did."

Hayes snapped three photos—the first of Lucky crawling on the ledge, the second of him falling in midair, and the third of the cat after landing on a cement balcony on the sixth floor. "I didn't know if it was dead or alive," Hayes said. "I found him curled up on a [charcoal] grill cover."

Lucky was rushed to a vet, where he was treated for minor injuries—a broken toe and a broken lower jaw.

"He's incredible," said Hostetler. "He's just an amazing cat."

Surprisingly, cats actually have a better chance of escaping serious injury when falling from higher up because once they reach maximum speed, known as terminal velocity, their bodies relax and they are less likely to suffer broken bones. It also gives them more time to twist in midair and position themselves to land on their feet.

Cats have what is called a "righting reflex." They will instinctively turn in midair, using their tails for balance, which enables them to land on their feet. Cats will usually come down with their front paws first, just before the hind legs touch down, so that their pads absorb much of the impact.

THAT FIRST STEP CAN BE A KILLER

Paco the dog took one misstep—and plunged 11 stories from a condominium balcony. Amazingly, the next day the pooch was greeting visitors as though nothing had happened.

"It was quite a feat," declared owner Frank Woods, of New Smyrna Beach, Florida. "We began calling him 'Wonder Dog.'"

One day in 1993, the fluffy, white, ten-year-old bichon frise, who was virtually blind from cataracts, was lounging with Woods on the balcony of his oceanside condominium. But while sniffing the sea air, Paco stepped through a balcony railing to what Woods feared was certain death. "I saw the tail go over," recalled Woods. "I thought it was all over then."

The 15-pound dog slammed onto his side when he hit the ground. Fortunately, the soil had been softened by a recent heavy rain. To the surprise of condo residents who witnessed Paco's plunge, the pooch was still alive.

They quickly sought the help of Volusia County lifeguards Mark Brown and Curt Szabo, who were nearby. "I'm a canine lover myself, so I thought we'd do what we could to help him," Brown told reporters.

The lifeguards fashioned a stretcher from a leg splint meant for humans.

Then Woods took Paco to Dr. Andy Mozlin at the Smyrna Veterinary Hospital. Despite the 110-foot fall, the dog suffered nothing more than a broken leg and a bruised bladder. He was treated and released eight hours after the accident. "He landed on his side, so that spread the impact out," explained Dr. Mozlin. "It's incredible, but he left here with his tail wagging."

Added Brown, "Especially since he's blind, Paco must have gotten a heck of a rush dropping eleven floors."

HEADING FOR A FALL

One minute Laddy the springer spaniel was walking along the edge of a seaside cliff with his master, and the next moment the dog disappeared without a trace.

Not until eight days later did anyone discover what had happened to him: Laddy had fallen 130 feet off the cliff and lived. But he was trapped on a rocky ledge that could only be seen from the ocean.

His ordeal began when he and his master, George Williamson, of Antrim, Northern Ireland, were on a hike in 2010 on the north Antrim coast. Somehow, the two-and-a-half-year-old dog lost his footing and tumbled over the cliff.

"Laddy knows every inch of where he was walking," Williamson's grandson, Connor Donnelly, told the *Belfast Telegraph*. "We don't know how he fell. He just vanished. We looked all over the cliff, calling and calling his name, but he was so far down we couldn't hear him and he couldn't hear us. You wouldn't know how he fell. It was very high."

Laddy's devastated family put up "Lost Dog" posters around the town of Ballycastle after he went missing. Though determined not to leave the area without Laddy, the dog's owners began to give up hope after a week went by without any word about the spaniel's fate.

On the eighth day since the dog's disappearance, a yachtsman spotted Laddy out on wave-swept rocks near a cave on the side of the cliff at Claire Park, Ballycastle. He tried coaxing the dog to swim out to his boat, but Laddy resisted. The man then called the coast guard, which rushed to the scene.

When they arrived at the top of the cliff, they set up their equipment and lowered a rescuer, known as a cliff technician, about 130 feet down to where Laddy was trapped. Gordon Munro, sector manager with

Her Majesty's Coast Guard, told reporters, "My cliff technician did very well to get this dog into the harness and winch it back to the top of the cliff because it was such a long drop.

"The dog was barking away and looked really pleased to see his owner. It is truly a miracle that this dog survived this cliff fall."

Despite plunging so far down, Laddy suffered minor injuries to his paw and front legs and was hungry and dehydrated.

"He was very dehydrated because he wouldn't drink the seawater," Donnelly told the newspaper. "We don't know how he survived, but we are so glad he did."

About the Author

Allan Zullo is the author of more than 100 nonfiction books on subjects ranging from sports and the supernatural to history and animals.

He has written the bestselling Haunted Kids series, published by Scholastic, which are filled with chilling stories based on, or inspired by, documented cases from the files of ghost hunters. Allan also has introduced Scholastic readers to the Ten True Tales series, about people who have met the challenges of dangerous, sometimes life-threatening, situations. He is the author of such animal books as *Incredible Dogs and Their Incredible Tales*, *True Tales of Animal Heroes*, and *Bad Pets: True Tales of Misbehaving Animals*. Allan, the grandfather of five and the father of two grown daughters, lives with his wife, Kathryn, on the side of a mountain near Asheville, North Carolina. To learn more about the author, visit his Web site at www.allanzullo.com.